Number, Pattern and Calculating 3
Explore More Copymasters

Written and developed by
Val Willmott

OXFORD

OXFORD
UNIVERSITY PRESS

Great Clarendon Street, Oxford, OX2 6DP, United Kingdom

Oxford University Press is a department of the University of Oxford.
It furthers the University's objective of excellence in research, scholarship,
and education by publishing worldwide. Oxford is a registered trade mark
of Oxford University Press in the UK and in certain other countries.

© Oxford University Press 2014

The moral rights of the author have been asserted

First Edition published in 2014

Photocopying

ISBN 978-0-19-838974-3

10 9 8 7 6 5 4 3 2 1

Typeset by Tech-Set Ltd, Gateshead

Paper used in the production of this book is a natural,
recyclable product made from wood grown in sustainable forests.
The manufacturing process conforms to the environmental regulations
of the country of origin.

Printed in Great Britain by Ashford Colour Press

Acknowledgements

Written and developed by Val Willmott

Cover artwork by David Semple

Figurative artwork by Matt Ward

Photographs by Jonty Tacon

With special thanks to Telscombe Cliffs Community Primary School,
Peacehaven

The authors and publisher would like to thank all schools and individuals
who have helped to trial and review Numicon resources.

www.oxfordprimary.co.uk/numicon

For teachers
Helping you with free eBooks, inspirational
resources, advice and support

For parents
Helping your child's learning
with free eBooks, essential
tips and fun activities

www.oxfordowl.co.uk

About Numicon

Numicon is a distinctive multi-sensory approach to children's
mathematical learning that emphasizes three key aspects of doing
mathematics: communicating mathematically, exploring relationships,
and generalizing.

Numicon was founded in the daily experience of intelligent children
having real difficulty with maths, the frequent underestimation of the
complexity of the ideas that young children are asked to face when
doing maths and recognition of the importance of maths to them and to
society as a whole.

Numicon aims to facilitate children's understanding and enjoyment of
maths by using structured imagery that plays to children's strong sense
of pattern. This is done through research-based, multi-sensory teaching
activities.

Numicon takes into account the complexity of abstract number ideas
and seeks to foster the self-belief necessary to achieve in the face of
challenge or difficulty.

Through the combination of communicating mathematically
(being active, talking and illustrating), exploring relationships
and generalizing, children are given the support to structure their
experiences: a vital skill for both their mathematical and their overall
development.

A multi-sensory approach, particularly one that makes use of structured
imagery, provides learners with the opportunity to play to their
strengths, thereby releasing their potential to enjoy, understand and
achieve in maths. By watching and listening to what children do
and say, this enjoyment in achievement is also shared by teachers
and parents.

Numicon strives to support teachers' subject knowledge and pedagogy
by providing teaching materials, Professional Development and
on-going support that will help develop a better understanding of
how to encourage all learners in the vital early stages of their own
mathematical journey.

Contents

Explore More Copymasters

The Explore More Copymasters have been designed to give children one practice activity to do at home for each activity group in the Number, Pattern and Calculating 3 teaching programme. As such, there are 30 homework activities within this book.

In order to support parents and carers as they help children with these activities, you might want to hold a short meeting to explain what Numicon is and what is expected of the homework.

Ahead of this meeting, you might want to print or photocopy Numicon Shapes 1–10 and Numicon 10-shapes (pp. 66 and 67) onto card, laminate them and give one set to each parent or carer for them to cut out and keep at home. These resources are used in a lot of the activities and having a set at home would really help children to take their learning out of the classroom.

You may also want to consider sending home a copy of the Numicon Table Top Number Line for parents and carers to display at home.

On the following page, there is a guidance letter to send home to parents and carers giving them more details about how they can play an active role helping their child with their maths learning, explaining about the special equipment that Numicon makes use of and giving them an idea of roughly how long activities will take.

You can add your own information to this letter touching upon some of the administrative details that are relevant to your school, e.g. the day homework will be sent home, when it should be returned and what parents and carers should do if they have further questions.

The letter also refers parents and carers to the Numicon website to find out more about Numicon. It also refers parents and carers to the Oxford Owl website for more general help and advice that might be useful for them.

Dear Parent/Guardian

The children in our school are learning maths using Numicon.

Numicon is a method of teaching maths that uses concrete resources to give children a picture of number ideas. We find that this approach helps all children to succeed. We will be sending home a piece of homework each week over the school year so that you can support your child as they practise the maths they have been learning at school.

How can I help my child with maths?

As adults, it's easy to forget how long it took us when we were children to understand maths ideas, so we tend to think they are simple. However, to a child, they are not simple and it often takes time and lots of practice to understand them.

You are not expected to teach your child these ideas, but you can help by making sure your child knows what to do and discuss their ideas with them.

To help you understand the purpose of each piece of homework, the maths involved in each activity is explained on a sheet of paper for you. This sheet includes: information on how the activity will help your child; words and phrases that your child is learning in their maths lessons; what to look for as your child does the activity; what you will need and what to do in order to complete the activity. There are also some 'Next steps…' suggestions if you want to extend the practice further.

Will I need any special equipment?

Many of the homework activities involve children handling and moving **Numicon Shapes**, so we will be sending home a set of laminated card Numicon Shapes 1–10, and extra card Numicon 10-shapes for you to cut out and keep at home.

Other activities involve household items, e.g. buttons, a dice, 1p, 2p, 5p and 10p coins.

How long will it take?

The homework activity will take between ten and twenty minutes once a week. There are also suggestions of other things you can do to extend the homework idea. Some of these are solving word problems, or playing a game. There are also suggestions of things to look out for and talk about around the home or when out and about.

If you would like to find out more about helping your child as they learn maths, www.oxfordowl.co.uk has some help and advice for parents.

To find out more about Numicon, visit the Numicon website: www.oxfordprimary.co.uk/numicon where there are short videos explaining the background to Numicon and how to use it.

Yours sincerely

Talk Time

How this will help your child

- This activity will allow your child to link the Numicon Shapes to numbers.
- It will help them to talk about the Shapes.
- It will give them a chance to see how the Shapes relate to each other.

Words and phrases to use

before, after, between, more, fewer, nearly, half, double, together

You will need

- Card Numicon Shapes 1–10
- 11 counters or buttons

During the activity, look at what your child can do

- Recognize the Shapes and give them number names.
- Talk about how the Shapes relate to each other.

What to do

- Give your child the Talk Time sheet and their card Numicon Shapes.
- Ask them to put the Shapes in order from 1 to 10 along the empty number line. **1**
- Read through all the speech bubbles with your child.
- Ask them to choose a Shape to play the game with, e.g. the 3-shape.
- Your child should then choose a speech bubble and use it to talk about their chosen Shape, e.g. 'It is two more than 1.'
- If they are correct, they can put a counter on that speech bubble. **2**
- Choose a different speech bubble for you to talk about the same Shape.
- If your child says you are correct and they are right, put a counter on that speech bubble.
- Play together to cover as many speech bubbles as possible for that Shape.
- The empty speech bubble can be used to make a new sentence. **3**
- Repeat for other Shapes.

> ### Next steps…
> - Play the same game with the number line covered.
> - Choose a Shape, but don't say which Shape you have chosen. Your child can use the speech bubbles to ask questions to work out the number of the Shape, e.g. 'Is it in between 2 and 6?'

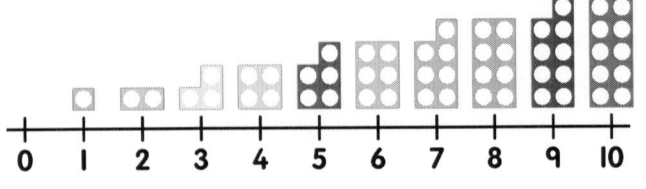

1

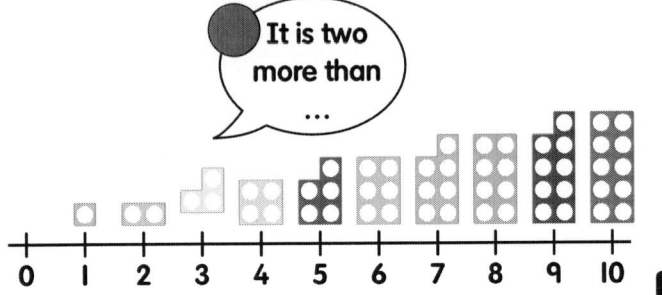

It is two more than …

2

If we take it away from the …-shape, we get the …-shape.

3

Talk Time

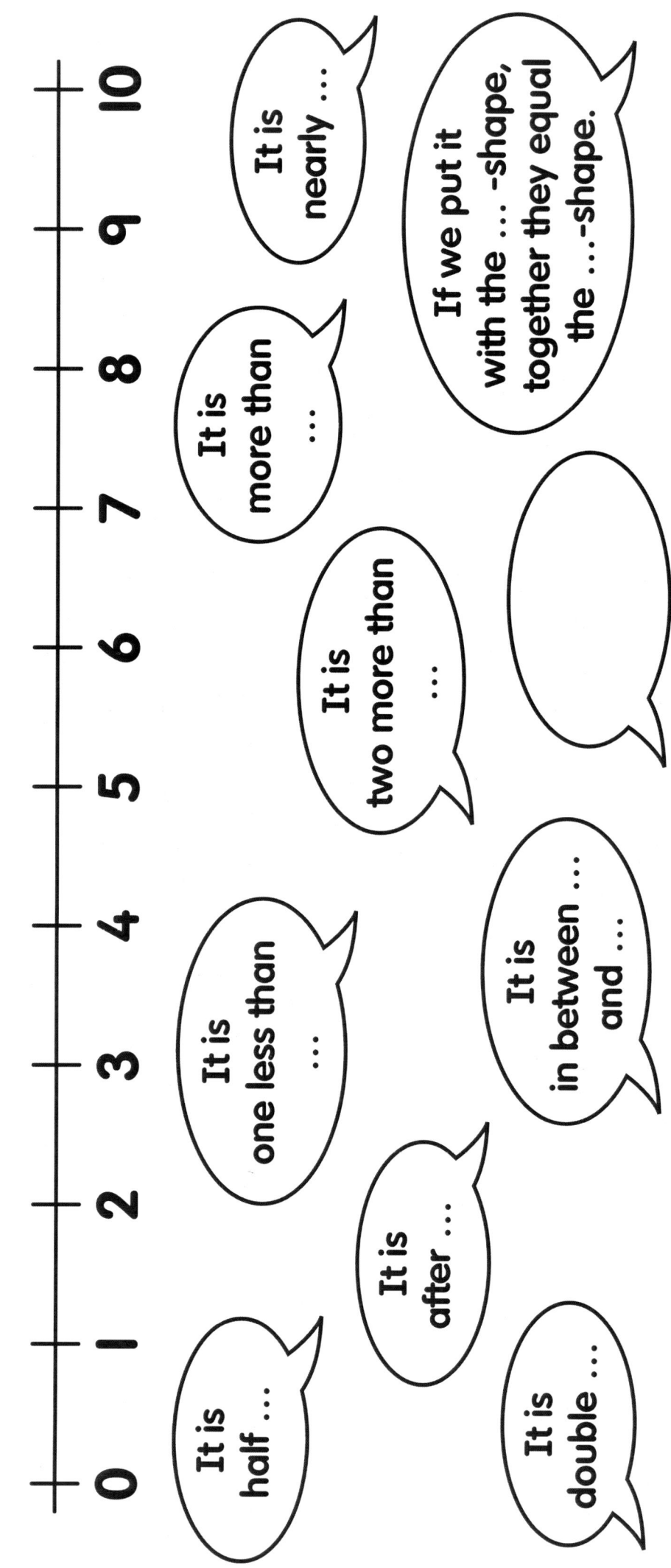

Pattern and Algebra 1, Exploring the inverse relationship between adding and subtracting

Number Trios

How this will help your child

- This activity will allow your child to explore connections between 3 numbers.
- It will help them to understand the phrase 'number trio'.
- It will give them a chance to practise using maths words, e.g. add, subtract, equals.

Words and phrases to use

number trio, add, subtract, equals

You will need

- 10 counters or small coins
- A paper clip
- A pencil
- An eraser

During the activity, look at what your child can do

- Show you how numbers are part of another whole number, e.g. 3 and 4 are both part of 7.
- Use maths words to describe number trios.

What to do

- Make the spinner on the Number Trios sheet using the paper clip and pencil. Place the paper clip over the centre spot of the spinner. Push the tip of the pencil through the centre spot and hold it in place as you spin the paper clip.
- Ask your child to spin the paper clip to choose a Numicon Shape, e.g. 7.
- Show your child the 10-pattern outline from the Number Trios sheet and ask them to build the Numicon Shape pattern for the Shape using counters or small coins. **1**
- Show your child the number trio template and ask them to write this number in the top circle of the trio. **2**
- Ask them to write two numbers that could go in the bottom two circles to make a number trio, e.g. 3 and 4. **3**
- Ask them to describe their number trio to you using maths words, e.g. '3 add 4 equals 7, 7 take away 3 equals 4.'
- Erase the first number trio and encourage your child to find more, e.g. 7, 2, 5 and 7, 1, 6.
- Spin again to choose another number and repeat.

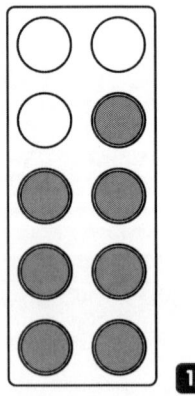

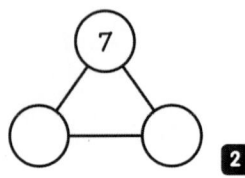

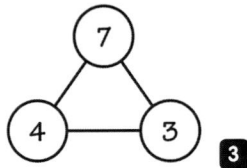

> ## Next steps…
>
> - Use objects, such as toy cars or books, and arrange them in Numicon Shape patterns. Ask number trio questions, e.g. 'There are 8 books on the shelf. If we read 2, how many do we have left to read?'
> - Pick a number trio, e.g. 6, 2, 4, and ask your child to write all the related adding and subtracting facts: $2 + 4 = 6$, $4 + 2 = 6$, $6 - 4 = 2$, $6 - 2 = 4$

Number Trios

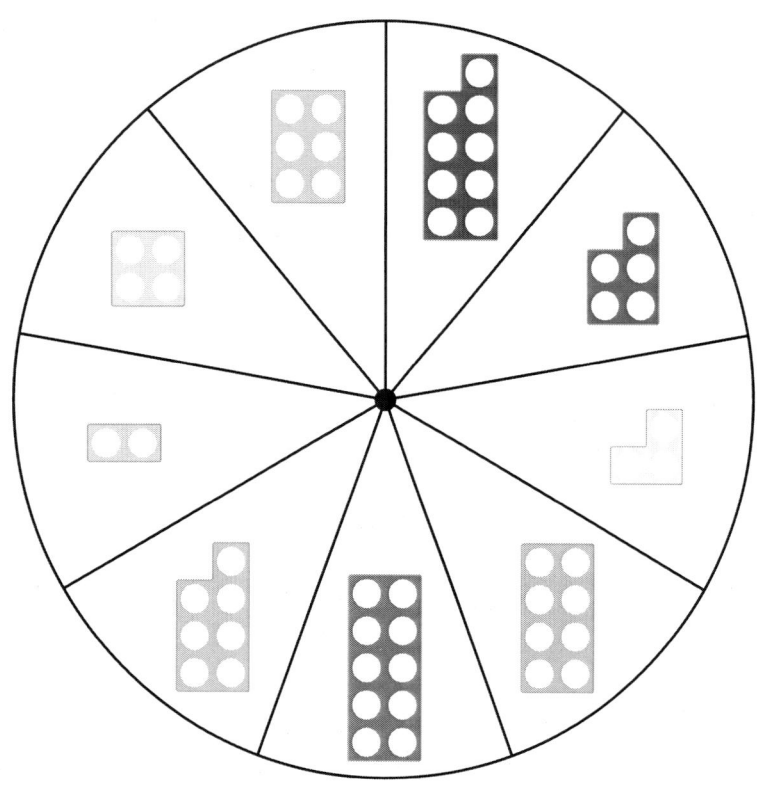

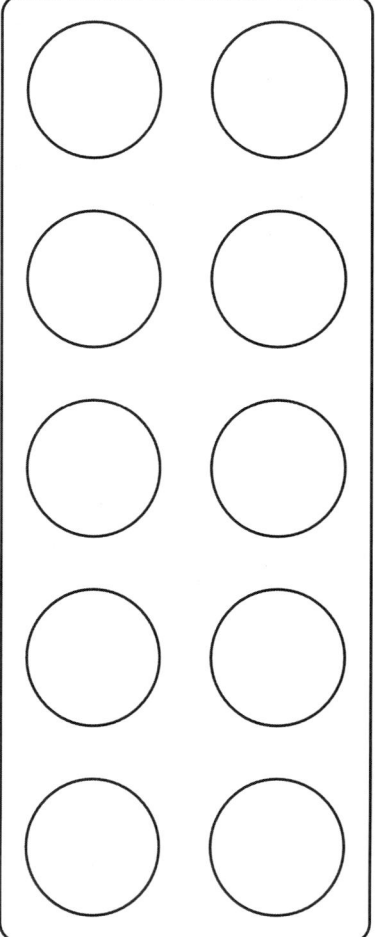

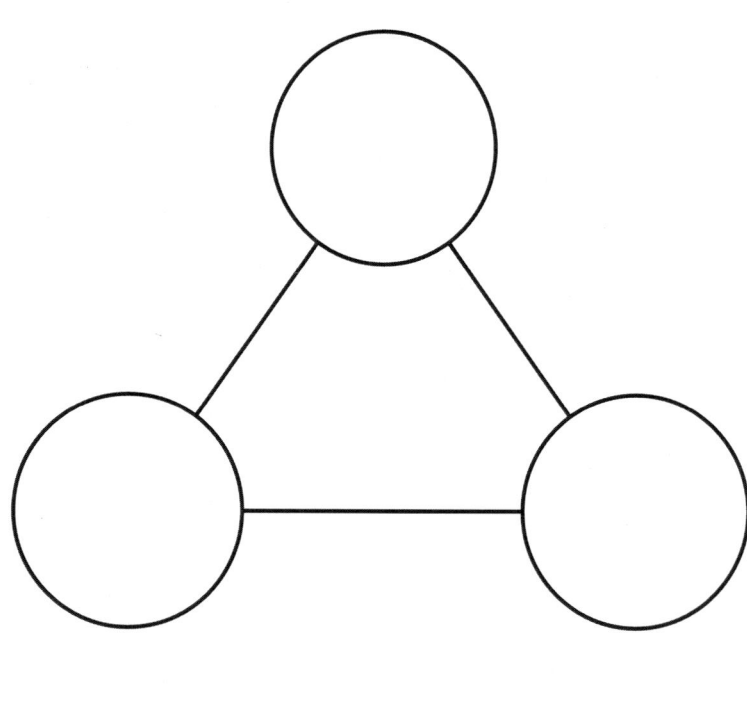

Pattern and Algebra 2, Exploring steps of constant size through sequences of multiples

Three In A Row

How this will help your child

- This activity will allow your child to practise counting aloud in 2s and hearing the patterns in the words.
- It will help them to identify multiples of 2 that are next to each other.
- It will give them a chance to spot gaps in a sequence.

Words and phrases to use

increasing by 2, decreasing by 2, multiple, sequence

You will need

- 1–6 dice
- Counters or buttons in 2 colours (one colour for each player)

During the activity, look at what your child can do

- Identify a sequence of multiples of 2, starting from different numbers.
- Spot gaps in sequences when counting in 2s.

What to do

- Give your child the Three In A Row sheet and ask them to talk about any patterns they can see on the grid, e.g. all the rows start with a tens number.
- Decide who is going to play first.
- The first player rolls the dice. The number shown gives you the tens number on the grid.
- The first player puts one of their coloured counters on any multiple of 2 in that row, e.g. if 1 is rolled, the player can choose 10, 12, 14, 16 or 18. **1**
- Take it in turns to roll the dice and place counters on multiples of 2. If there are no numbers left on a row, the player misses a turn.
- The winner is the first person to place 3 counters in an uninterrupted sequence within a row. **2**
- Ask your child to say the winning sequence of multiples of 2 out loud, forwards and backwards.
- Play again with the other player starting first.

> ### Next steps…
> - Change the rules of the game so that the 3 winning counters can go over two rows, e.g. 38, 40 and 42.
> - Count objects found at home using the multiples of 2 sequence, e.g. socks, shoes, gloves.

1

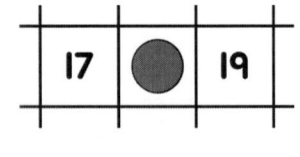

2

Name ....

Date .... / .... / ....

Three In A Row

10	11	12	13	14	15	16	17	18	19
20	21	22	23	24	25	26	27	28	29
30	31	32	33	34	35	36	37	38	39
40	41	42	43	44	45	46	47	48	49
50	51	52	53	54	55	56	57	58	59
60	61	62	63	64	65	66	67	68	69

Number, Pattern and Calculating 3
Pattern and Algebra 2, Exploring steps of constant size through sequences of multiples

Broken Ruler

How this will help your child

- This activity will allow your child to use their knowledge of counting in 5s to label a scale.
- It will help them to read a scale where not all the numbers are marked.

Words and phrases to use

scale, sequence, multiple, interval, in between

You will need

- Scissors

During the activity, look at what your child can do

- Count forwards and backwards in 5s.
- Find missing numbers on a scale using their knowledge of number patterns.

What to do

- Cut out the numeral cards from the Broken Ruler sheet and place them face up, in order.
- Ask your child to look at the sequence of numbers, 15–80, and say them out loud, both forwards and backwards.
- Shuffle the cards and spread them out face down.
- Give your child the Broken Ruler sheet.
- Ask your child to pick one of the cards and place it on the middle of the broken ruler over the question mark. **1**
- Ask them to complete the remaining missing numbers by picking another card and seeing if it fits anywhere on the scale. **2**
- If your child cannot find the correct card, ask them to say or write the number they think should go in the space.
- Continue until the scale shows seven correct numbers.
- Repeat with a different number in the middle of the broken ruler.

> ### Next steps…
> - Challenge your child to find numbers on the broken ruler scale using the smaller intervals, e.g. find 36 or 34 if the middle number on the broken ruler is 35.
> - Go on a 'scale hunt' around your home. How many different scales can your child find? What are they used for? Talk about the intervals on the scales and what numbers they show.

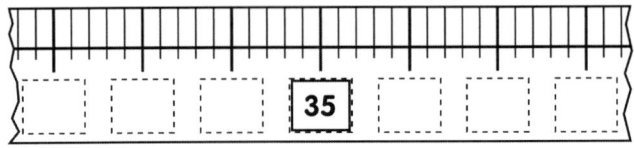

1

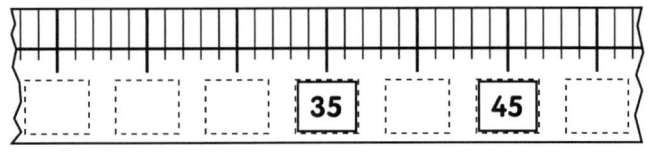

2

Name ....

Date .... / .... / ....

Broken Ruler

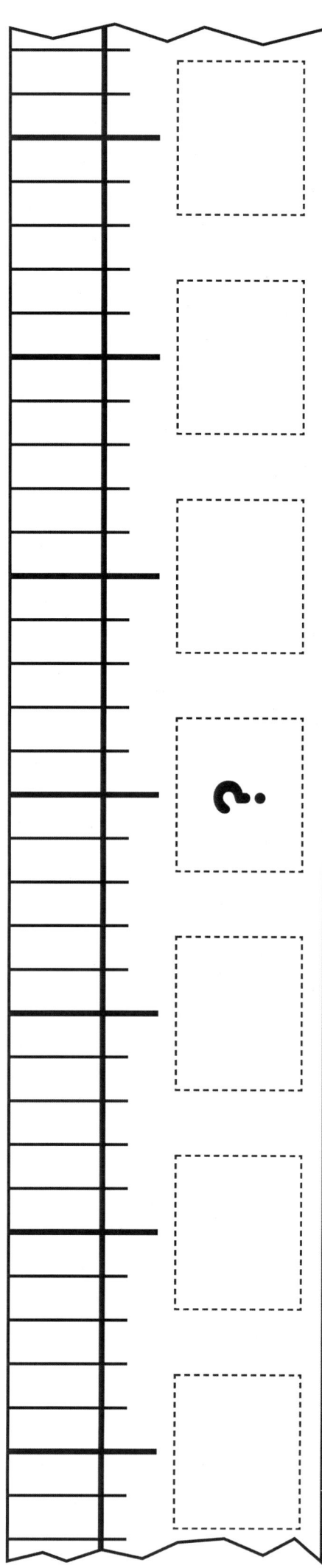

?

| 15 | 20 | 25 | 30 | 35 | 40 | 45 |
| 50 | 55 | 60 | 65 | 70 | 75 | 80 |

Number, Pattern and Calculating 3
Pattern and Algebra 3, Reading and creating scales with different intervals

4

Pattern and Algebra 4, Extending sequences and finding differences

Snake Sequences

How this will help your child

- This activity will help your child to follow rules to make number sequences.
- It will allow them to notice patterns in sequences.
- It will give them a chance to explain these patterns.

Words and phrases to use

sequence, pattern, difference, odd, even

You will need

- A paper clip
- A pencil

During the activity, look at what your child can do

- Create number sequences by following a rule.
- Describe the sequence using maths words.

What to do

- Give your child the Snake Sequences sheet and explain that, together, you are going to make your own number sequences.
- Make the spinner on the Snake Sequences sheet using a paper clip and pencil. Place the paper clip over the centre spot of the spinner. Push the tip of the pencil through the centre spot and hold it in place as you spin the paper clip.
- Spin the paper clip to land on a number instruction. This is the number to add each time to make the sequence on the first snake, e.g. 1 add 2 makes 3, 3 add 2 equals 5. **1**
- Before finishing the sequence, ask your child to predict the number they think will be on the snake's head.
- See if they can describe the pattern in the sequence.
- Spin again to complete the sequence on the next snake.
- For the other snakes, your child can choose their own starting numbers. **2**

> ### Next steps...
> - Read the sequences from each snake's head to its tail. Ask your child to explain the rules for these new sequences.
> - Find number sequences in everyday life, e.g. house numbers on a street or floors in a department store. Ask your child if they can tell you about the sequence.

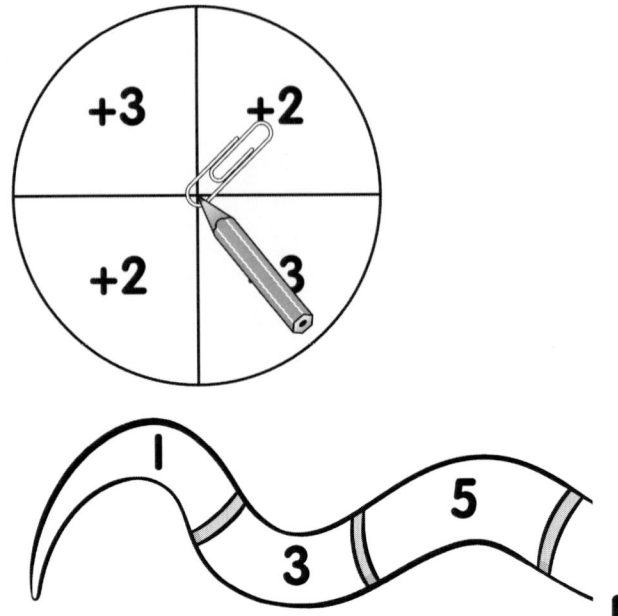

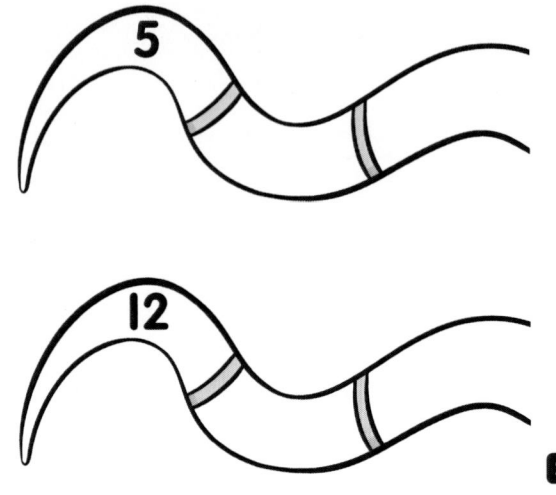

Name ....

Date .... / .... / ....

Snake Sequences

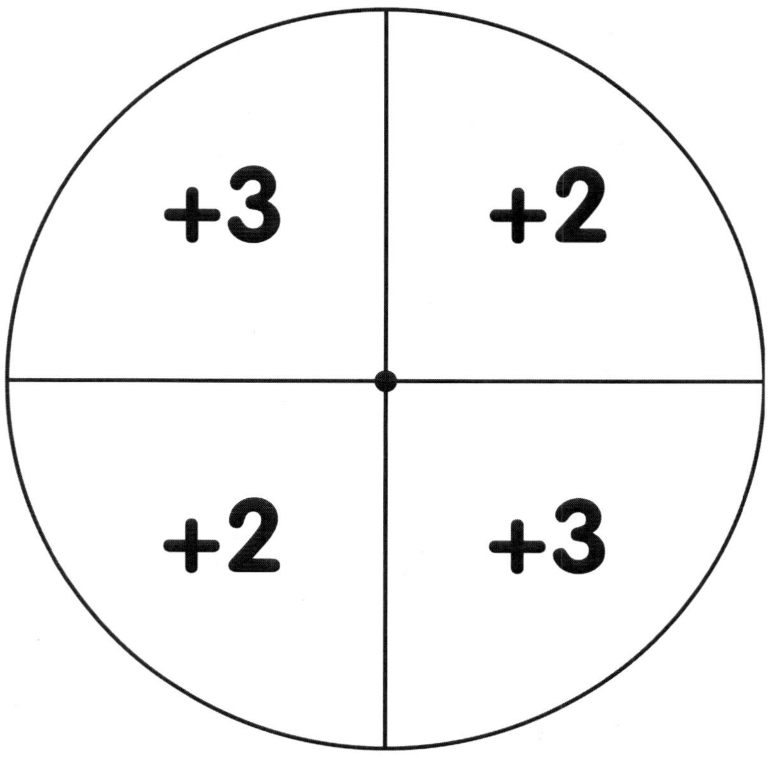

Pattern and Algebra 5, Finding all possibilities and investigating a general statement

Numicon Towers

How this will help your child

- This activity will show your child there can be more than one possible answer to a question.
- It will give them a way of organizing their ideas.
- It will help them to see how all possible answers could be found.

Words and phrases to use

total, list, same, all possibilities, organize, show, predict

You will need

- Card Numicon Shapes 1–10
- Colouring pencils

During the activity, look at what your child can do

- Look for patterns in the numbers.
- Record their ideas on paper.
- Organize their answers to find all possibilities.

What to do

- Give your child the Numicon Towers sheet and their card Numicon Shapes.
- Ask your child to use their Numicon Shapes to make Numicon towers of 10 with two different Shapes. How many different towers can they make?
- Explain that the order of the Shapes does not matter in this activity, so 3 and 7 make the same tower as 7 and 3.
- Encourage them to remove any towers that appear twice.
- They can use the Numicon Towers sheet to draw their ideas. **1**
- When they think they have found all the possibilities, ask them to find a way they could check, e.g. by starting with the smallest or largest number.
- Now ask your child to use the Shapes to make Numicon towers of 10 with three different Shapes. How many different towers can they make?
- Encourage them to draw their ideas on the empty Numicon towers. **2**

> ### Next steps…
> - What if the tower was 12 tall instead of 10? How many towers could be made if 2 different Shapes were used? Encourage your child to predict the totals before organizing the Shapes.
> - Decorate cakes and investigate the number of possible combinations with 2 flavours of icing and 2 different toppings. Or try 3 different pizza toppings.

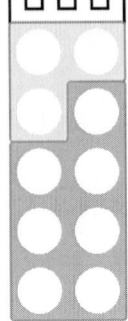

$3 + 7$ **1**

$2 + 1 + 7$ **2**

Name ....

Date .... / .... / ....

Numicon Towers

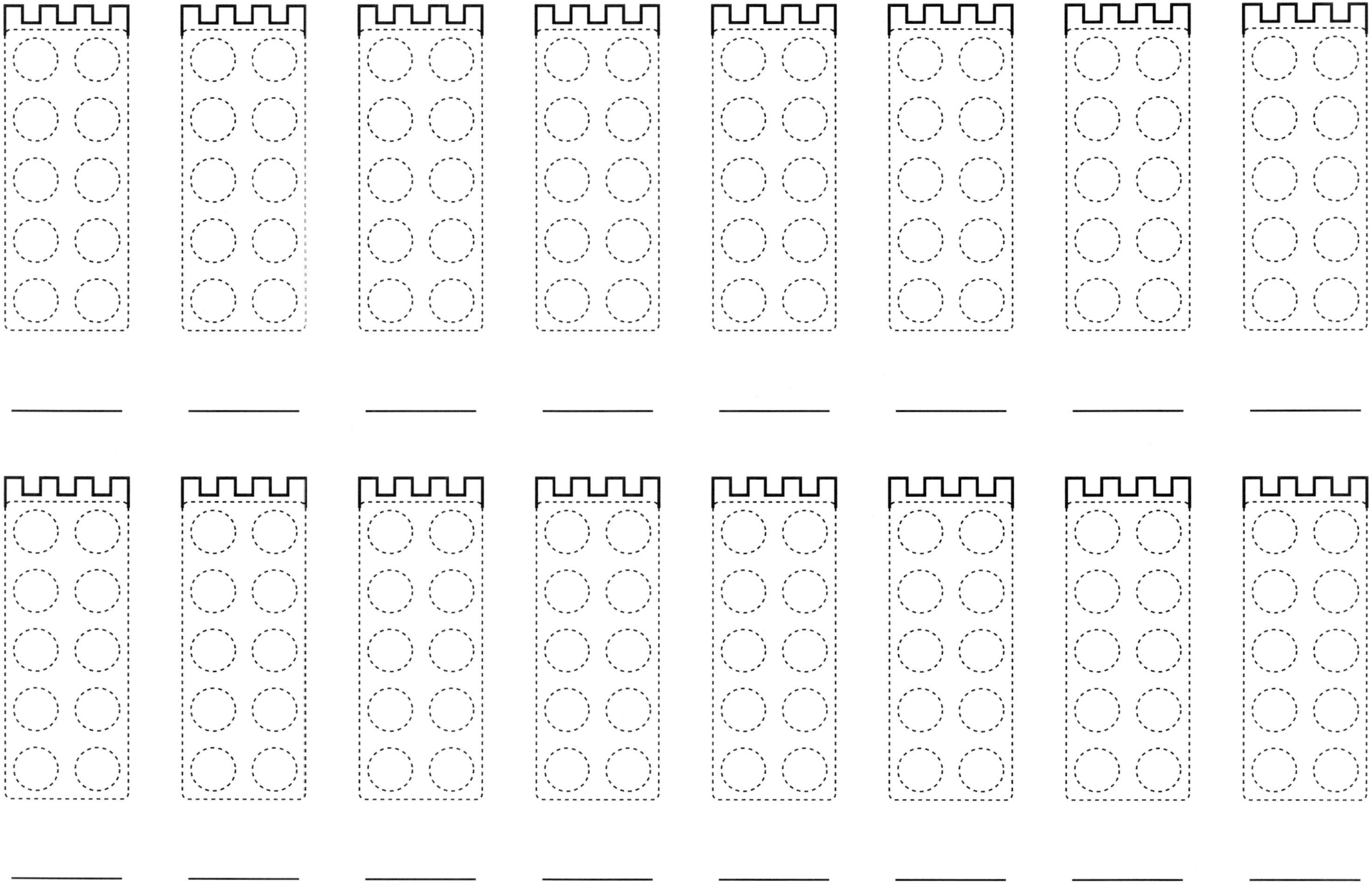

© Oxford University Press 2014. This page can be copied for use in the purchasing school.

Number, Pattern and Calculating 3
Pattern and Algebra 5, Finding all possibilities and investigating a general statement

Stars

How this will help your child

- This activity will allow your child to practise making sensible estimates of amounts larger than ten.
- It will help them to find out 'how many?' by grouping objects into tens and units.
- It will show them how this is linked to the tens and units in written numbers.

Words and phrases to use

estimate, guess, nearly, exactly, tens, units, groups, more, fewer

You will need

- Counters or buttons
- A pencil
- Scissors (optional)

During the activity, look at what your child can do

- Estimate 'how many?'
- Group objects in tens to find 'how many?'
- Write numbers to label groups of objects that have been counted.

What to do

- Give your child the Stars sheet.
- Ask your child to look at the four star cards and compare the number of stars on each card using words such as 'more' and 'fewer'.
- Ask them to estimate – without counting! – the number of stars on the first card. (You may want to cut out each card to separate them.)
- Next, cover each star on the first card with a counter. **1**
- Once each star has been covered, move the counters on to the table.
- Ask your child to use these counters to build Numicon 10-patterns, with any extra counters arranged into Numicon Shape patterns. **2**
- Discuss how many tens and units are in the number and ask your child to write it down, e.g. 17 has 1 ten and 7 units.
- Repeat with the other cards.

> ### Next steps…
> - Estimate how many stars are on 2 or 3 of the cards together.
> - Use collections of objects from around your home (coins, paper clips, greetings cards) to find out 'how many?' by estimating and then arranging them in Numicon Shape patterns.

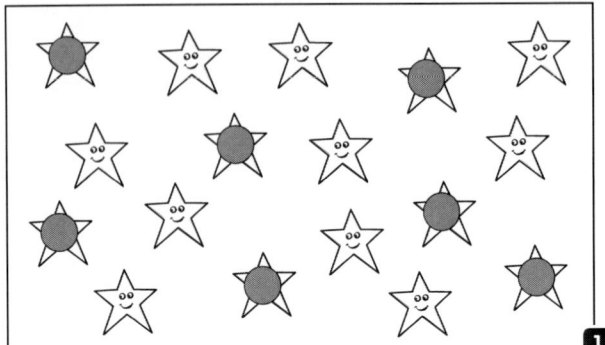

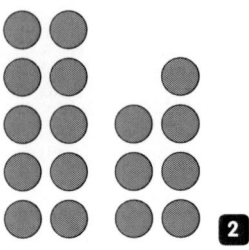

Name ....

Date .... / .... /

Stars

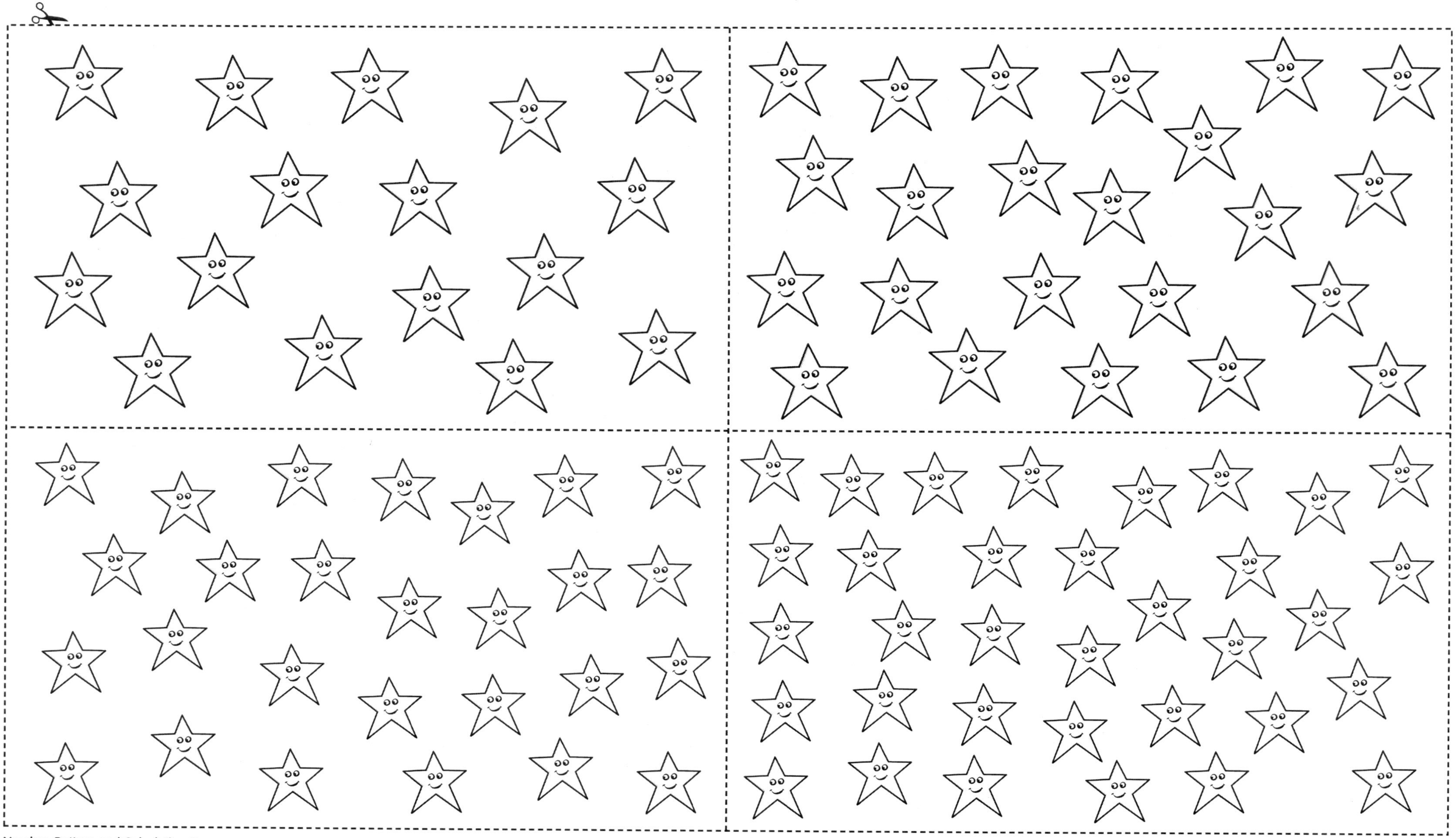

Number, Pattern and Calculating 3
Numbers and the Number System 1, Finding how many by grouping in 10s and 100s

Numbers and the Number System 2, Exploring hundreds, tens and units with base-ten apparatus

Robot Tens

How this will help your child

- This activity will allow your child to find 'how many?' by counting in groups of ten.

- It will help them to see how groups of ten are connected to written numbers, e.g. that 5 groups of 10 makes 50.

Words and phrases to use

tens, groups, more, predict

You will need

- A paper clip
- A pencil
- 20 counters or buttons
- Scissors

During the activity, look at what your child can do

- Count in tens up to 200.
- Use groups of ten to make tens numbers.
- Predict how many groups will be needed to make a tens number.

What to do

- Cut out the 20 robot cards from the Robot Tens sheet.

- Ask your child to count the number of blocks that have been used to make each robot. Make sure they know there are 10 blocks on each card.

- Make the spinner on the Robot Tens sheet using the paper clip and pencil. Place the paper clip over the centre spot of the spinner. Push the tip of the pencil through the centre spot and hold it in place as you spin the paper clip to land on a Numicon Shape 1–5.

- Your child should take that number of robot cards from the pile, e.g. if they land on a 4, they should take 4 cards from the pile. **1**

- Ask how many blocks have been used to make the robots on these cards, e.g. 4 robot cards are made from 40 blocks. Put a counter on this number on the cog number line. **2**

- Take turns to try and cover all numbers on the number line.

- For numbers over 50, you will need to collect cards from 2 or more spins.

> ### Next steps…
> - Use construction kits to make robot models from 10 blocks.
> - Look for 2-digit numbers in books, calendars and recipes and ask your child to tell you how many tens are in each number.

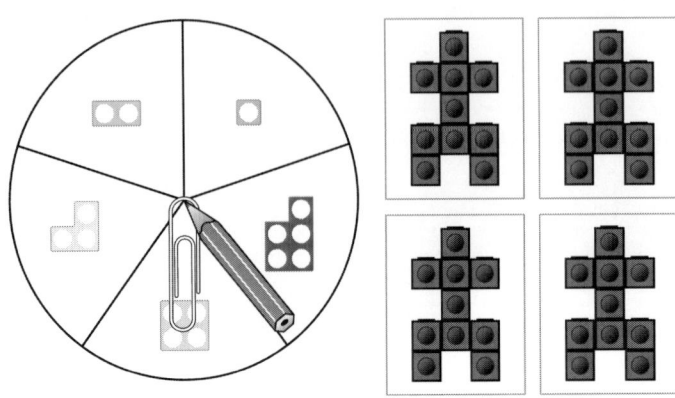

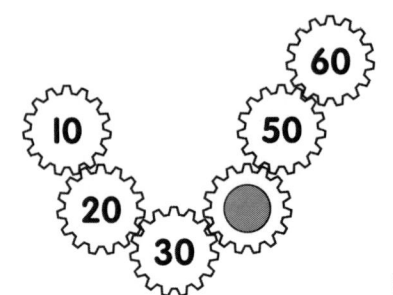

Name ....

Date .... / .... / ....

Robot Tens

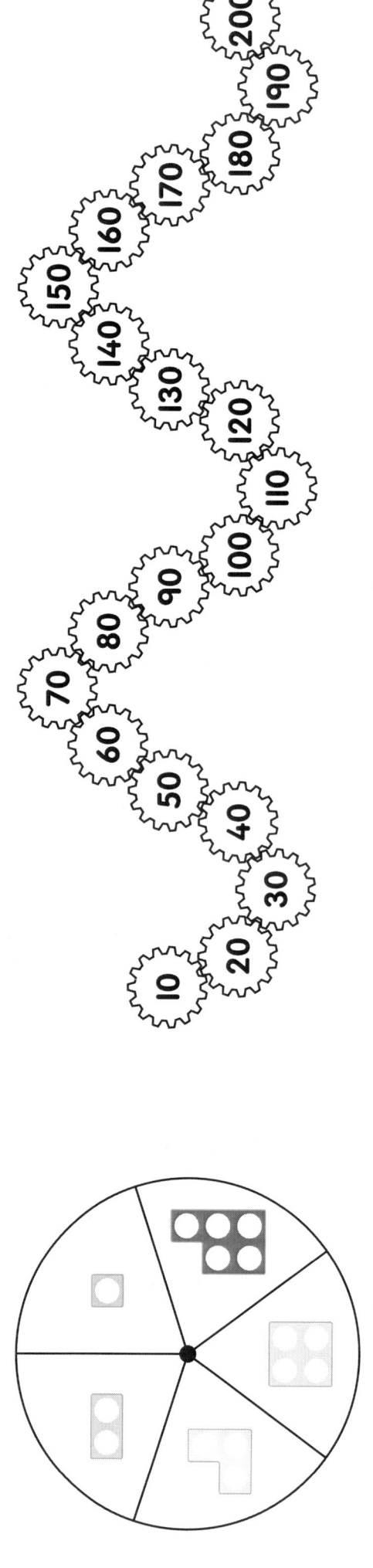

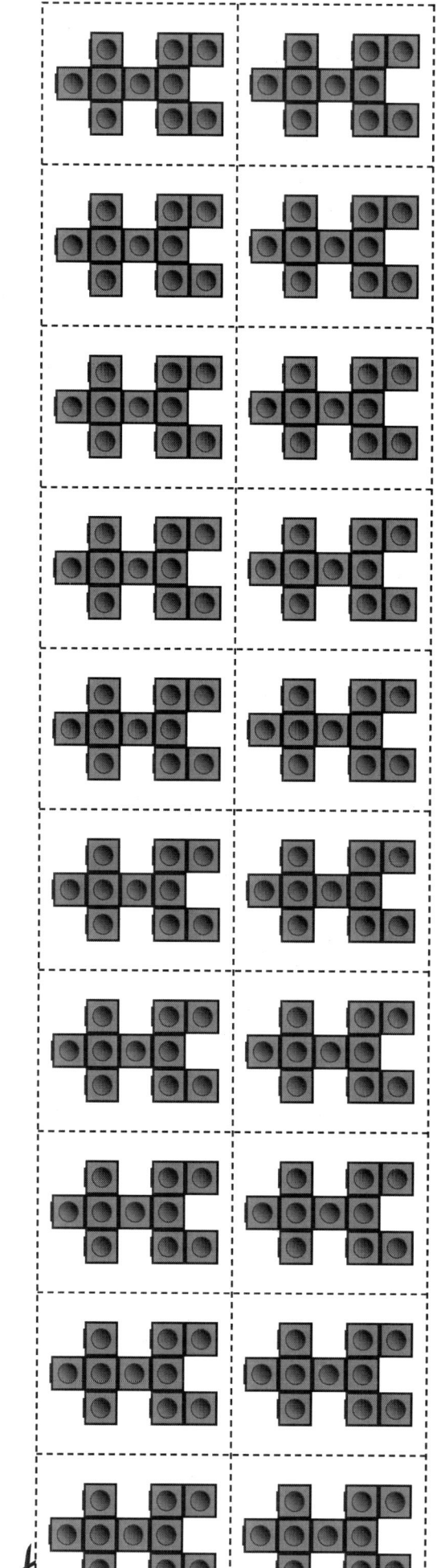

Numbers and the Number System 3, Keeping count and writing numbers down

Home Survey

How this will help your child

- This activity will encourage your child to look closely at intervals on a number line.
- It will give them a chance to practise counting things that move.
- It will help them to record using a 0–50 number line.

Words and phrases to use

survey, count, intervals, tens, units

You will need

- A pencil
- A clock

During the activity, look at what your child can do

- Work out intervals on a number line.
- Count and record things that move.

What to do

- Ask your child to think of things that move near your home, e.g. cars driving past, birds in the garden, and to choose one thing to count.
- Explain that, together, you're going to carry out a survey to find out how many things you can see in a set amount of time.
- Give your child the Home Survey sheet. Together, decide a length of time to look, e.g. 10 minutes.
- Show your child how to mark one interval on the number line every time they see one thing they are counting. **1**
- When the time is finished, ask your child to use the intervals on the number line to find out how many things you saw in the time.
- Write this final number on the recording sheet. **2**

Next steps...

- Carry out another survey when you are away from home, e.g. walk in a park and count the number of dogs, or walk through a shopping centre and count the number of people with green carrier bags. Your child can use the same sheet but record using a different colour, or you can just keep count of the things you see when you are out.

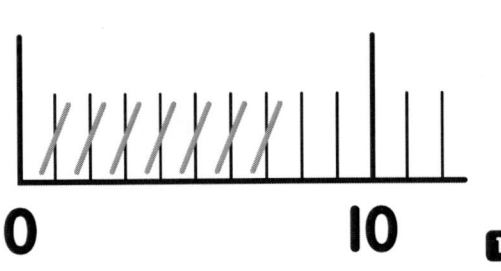

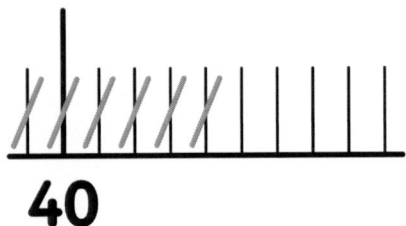

How many did you see? __44__ **2**

Name ....

Date .... / .... / ....

Home Survey

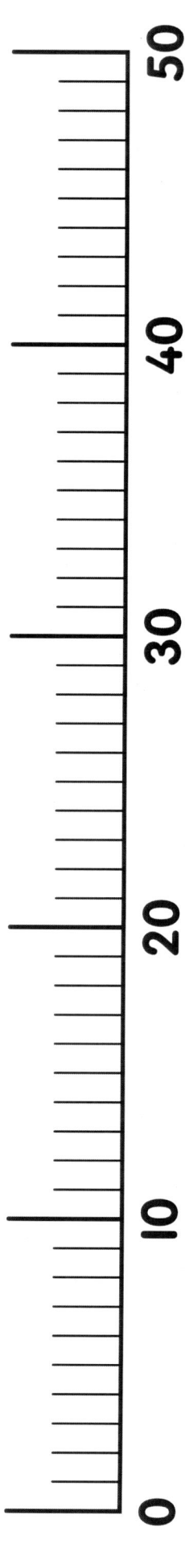

How many did you see? _____

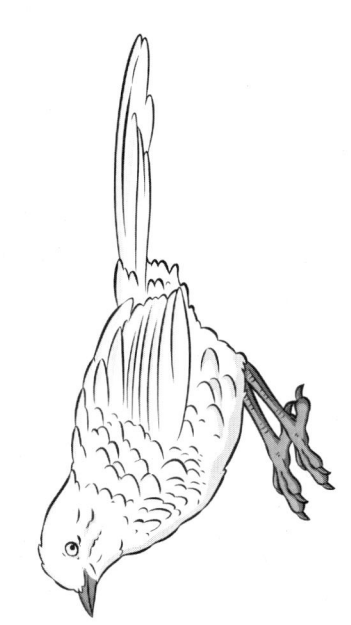

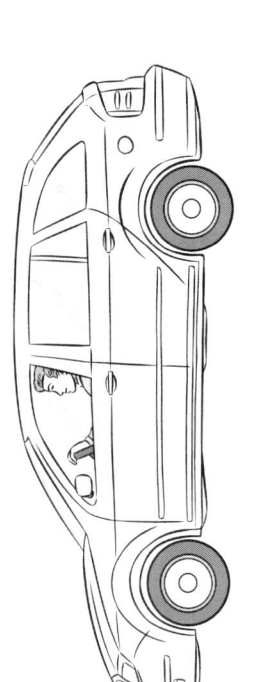

Number, Pattern and Calculating 3
Numbers and the Number System 3, Keeping count and writing numbers down

Numbers and the Number System 4, Partitioning 2- and 3-digit numbers with and without money

Game Show Prizes

How this will help your child

- This activity will give your child a chance to say and write 3-digit numbers.
- It will help them to know that the place of a digit in a number shows its value.
- It will allow them to practise splitting numbers into hundreds, tens and units.

Words and phrases to use

hundreds, tens, units, place, digit, value

You will need

- A paper clip
- A pencil

During the activity, look at what your child can do

- Read 3-digit numbers correctly out loud.
- Know the value of a digit from its place in a 3-digit number.
- Split 3-digit numbers in different ways.

What to do

- Give your child the Game Show Prizes sheet. Ask your child to imagine they have won a children's game show.
- Make the spinner on the Game Show Prizes sheet using a paper clip and pencil. Place the paper clip over the centre spot of the spinner. Push the tip of the pencil through the centre spot and hold it in place as you spin the paper clip.
- Ask your child to spin for a number. Write this digit in the Units box.
- Spin two more times to get a number for the Tens box and a number for the Hundreds box.
- Ask your child to say the 3-digit number, e.g. 'five hundred and sixty two'. **1**
- This is the number of points your child can use to claim their prizes from the game sheet.
- Ask your child to choose their prizes and to write down how they have worked out which prizes they can have. They should aim to use all their points. **2**
- Encourage them to work out how to get different prizes from the same number.
- Repeat the activity, using the spinner to create a new number for you to choose prizes.
- Who ended up with the largest number of prizes?

Next steps…

- Ask your child which prizes they would like to win before they spin for the number. How many points do they need? Encourage them to think about a good place to put each digit in order to reach that number of points.

Hundreds	Tens	Units
5	6	2

1

Hundreds	Tens	Units
5	6	2

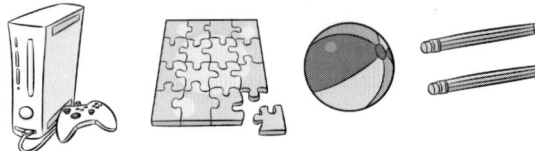

2

Game Show Prizes

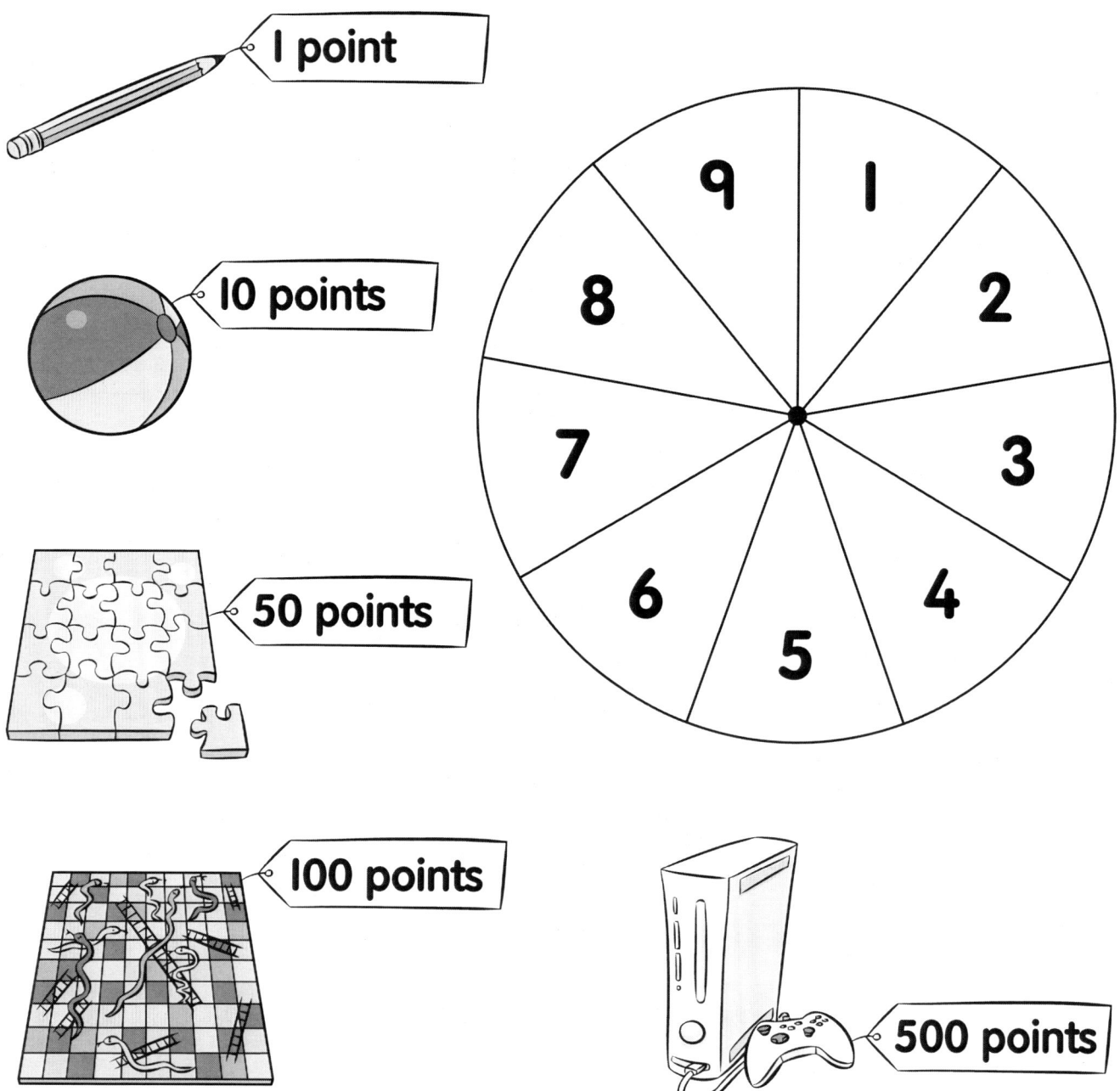

I point

10 points

50 points

100 points

500 points

Hundreds	Tens	Units

Numbers and the Number System 5, Ordering and structuring numbers to 1000

Jigsaw 100

How this will help your child

- This activity will help your child to understand the layout of a 100 square.
- It will give them a chance to look for patterns in the numbers on a 100 square.
- It will help them to see how numbers from 1–100 relate to each other.

Words and phrases to use

tens, units, order, pattern, more, fewer, arrangement, above, below, next to

You will need

- Scissors
- Glue

During the activity, look at what your child can do

- Find numbers on a 100 square.
- See patterns in numbers up to 100.
- Arrange numbers on a 100 square.

What to do

- Give your child the Jigsaw 100 sheet and ask them to look at the 100 square.
- Talk about the numbers they can see and ask questions to help them understand the layout of the 100 square, e.g. 'Which number is next to 1?' You can point to the square you are talking about.
- Your child may like to write some of the numbers into the empty squares. They should not write all of the numbers. **1**
- Ask them to look at the jigsaw pieces on the Jigsaw 100 sheet. Do they know where any of the pieces fit?
- Encourage them to look for patterns in the numbers, e.g. 31, 41, 51... the tens go up 1 each time, but the units stay the same; 91, 92, 93... the tens stay the same, but the units go up by 1 each time.
- Help your child to cut out the jigsaw pieces and glue them in the correct places on the 100 square. **2**

Next steps...

- Colour in patterns on the 100 square, e.g. odd numbers or multiples of 5.
- Find numbers at home, for example, on calendars or food packaging. Ask your child to visualize the 100 square and describe where the number could be found, e.g. 72 is next to 71 and 73 and also above 82.

1					6		8	9	10
				15			18	19	20
				25			28	29	
				35					
				45					
				55					
				65					
71				75					
				85			88		
91	92	93	94	95	96	97	98		100

2

6	7			10
		18		

1

Name .... Date .... / .... / ....

Jigsaw 100

| 16 | 26 | 36 | 46 | 56 | 66 | 76 | 86 |

| 7 | 17 | 27 | 37 | 47 | 57 | 67 | 77 | 87 |

| 30 | 40 | 50 | 60 | 70 |

38	39
48	49
58	59
68	69

22	23	24
32	33	34
42	43	44
52	53	54

8	9	10
18	19	20
	29	

64	
72	73	74
82	83	84
81		

| 15 | 25 | 35 | 45 | 55 | 65 | 75 | 85 |

| 88 |
| 98 |

| 91 | 92 | 93 | 94 | 95 | 96 | 97 |
| | | | | | | |

2	3	4	5
12	13	14
11	21

78	79	80
89	90	
	99	

| 31 |
| 41 |
| 51 |
| 61 | 62 | 63 |

1				6					
		28							
71									
									100

Number, Pattern and Calculating 3
Numbers and the Number System 5, Ordering and structuring numbers to 1000

Running Track

How this will help your child

- This activity will give your child a chance to practise finding halfway between multiples of 10.
- It will help them to look for and recognize patterns in numbers.

Words and phrases to use

multiple, tens, exactly, halfway, between

You will need

- A pencil
- Scissors

During the activity, look at what your child can do

- Say halfway between multiples of 10.
- Recognize that numbers halfway between multiples of 10 end in 5.

What to do

- Cut out the 'halfway' cards from the Running Track sheet. Shuffle them and place them face down.
- Show your child the 100 metre running track from the Running Track sheet and ask them to label all the missing numbers on the side of the track with the correct multiples of 10. **1**
- Ask your child to tell you the number that is halfway between 0 and 10 metres and to point to it on the track.
- Ask your child to draw a short vertical line in the correct place and write the number 5 below the track. **2**
- Ask them to say the sentence in the speech bubble below the running track, including the missing numbers, e.g. 'The athlete runs halfway between 0 metres and 10 metres. They run 5 metres.'
- Take turns to pick a 'halfway' card, find that distance on the running track, draw the line on the track, write the number below it and complete the sentence.
- Continue until all the cards have been used.

> ### Next steps…
> - Give your child a number, e.g. 35, and ask them to tell you which 2 multiples of 10 it is halfway between. If possible, ask your child to do this without looking at the track.
> - Measure and cut lengths of string or wool that are exactly halfway between 2 multiples of 10, e.g. 15 cm long.

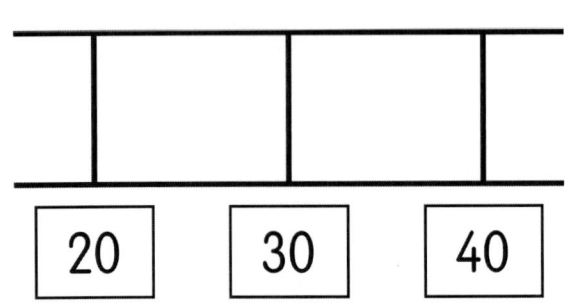

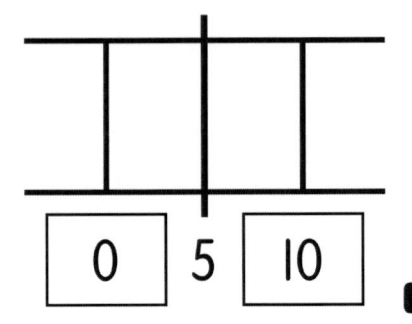

Name ....

Date .... / .... / ....

Running Track

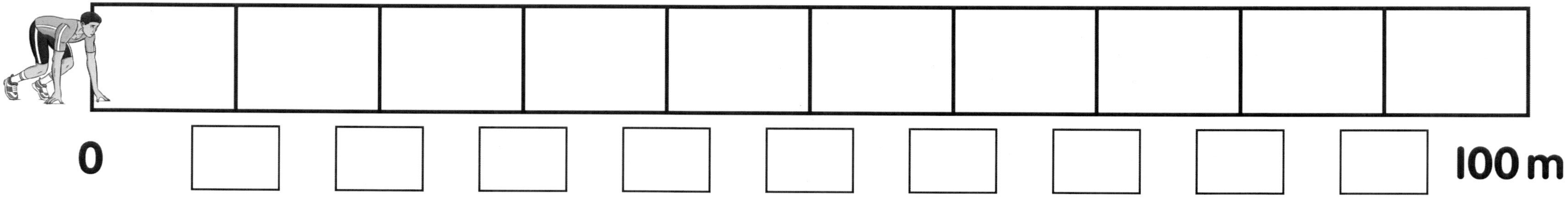

0   □   □   □   □   □   □   □   □   □   □   **100 m**

The athlete runs halfway
between _____ metres and _____ metres.
They run _____ metres.

halfway between 10 and 20 m	halfway between 20 and 30 m	halfway between 30 and 40 m	halfway between 40 and 50 m
halfway between 60 and 70 m	halfway between 70 and 80 m	halfway between 80 and 90 m	halfway between 90 and 100 m
halfway between 50 and 60 m			

Number, Pattern and Calculating 3
Numbers and the Number System 6, Finding halfway, rounding to the nearest 10 or 100

Numbers and the Number System 7, Understanding fractions of a whole and fractions as numbers

Fill The Squares

How this will help your child

- This activity will allow your child to practise reading fraction numbers and saying fraction names.
- It will help them to recognize fractions of whole squares.
- It will give them a chance to compare the size of some fractions.

Words and phrases to use

half, quarter, three quarters, parts, whole

You will need

- A paper clip
- A pencil
- Counters or buttons

During the activity, look at what your child can do

- Talk about fractions using the correct words.
- Recognize fractions of shapes.

What to do

- Give your child the Fill The Squares sheet. Ask them to look at the whole squares on the sheet and tell you how they have been divided into smaller parts.
- Now look at the spinner with your child. Ask them to say the fraction names for $\frac{1}{2}$ (one half), $\frac{1}{4}$ (one quarter) and $\frac{3}{4}$ (three quarters) out loud.
- Each player chooses a row of squares.
- Make the spinner on the Fill The Squares sheet using a paper clip and pencil. Place the paper clip over the centre spot of the spinner. Push the tip of the pencil through the centre spot and hold it in place as you spin the paper clip.
- Spin the spinner and cover that fraction of one of the squares with counters, e.g. $\frac{3}{4}$ can cover $\frac{1}{4}, \frac{1}{4}, \frac{1}{4}$. **1**
- If the spinner shows a fraction that is not available, the player misses a go.
- The winner is the first person to cover every part on all of their squares.
- Play the game again with the other player starting first.

> ### Next steps…
> - Repeat the game, allowing each player to make changes to the shapes and cover sections that are the same area, e.g. $\frac{3}{4}$. **2**
> - Use fractions words and phrases with your child in everyday activities, e.g. when folding towels, cutting sandwiches or sharing a birthday cake.

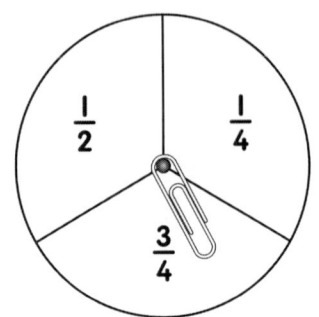

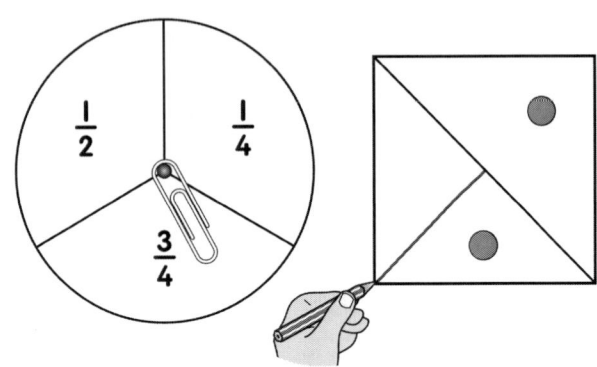

Name ....

Date .... / .... / ....

Fill The Squares

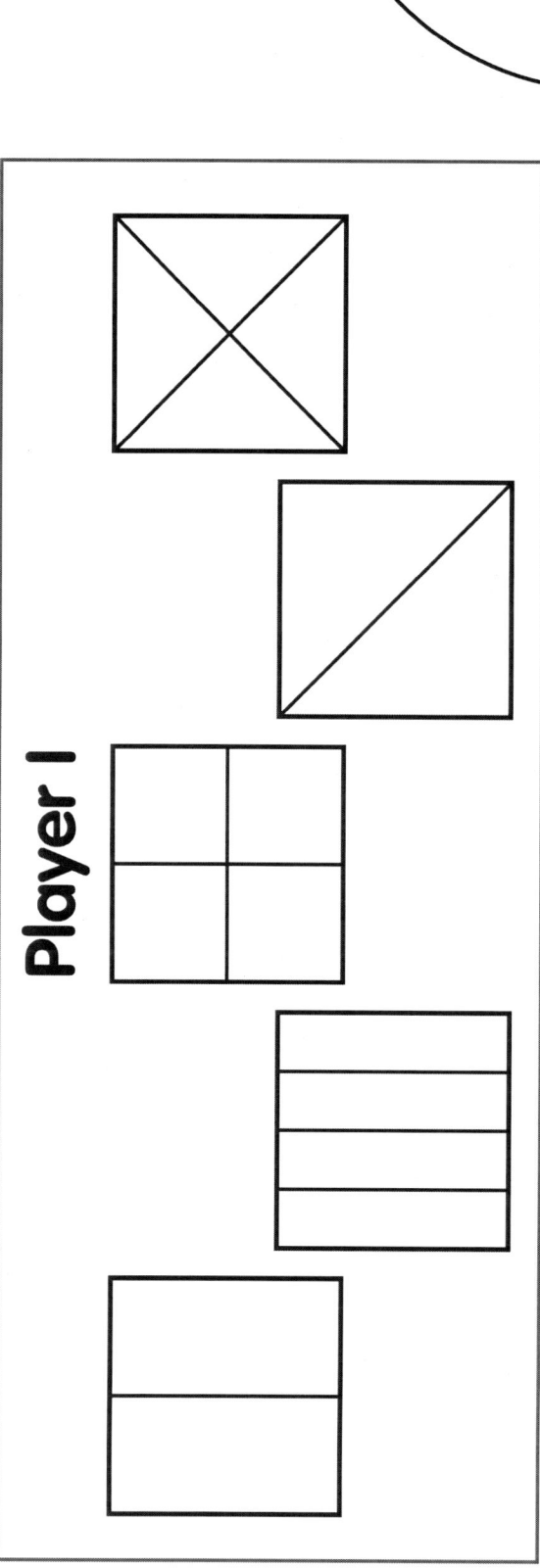

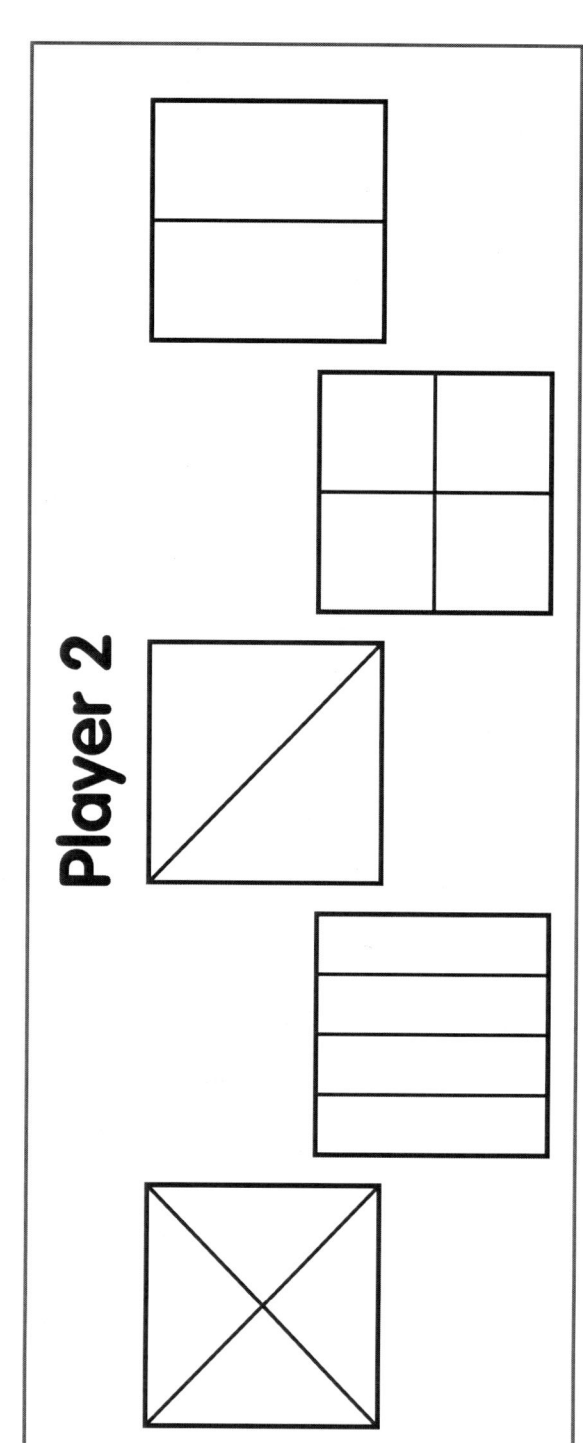

Number, Pattern and Calculating 3
Numbers and the Number System 7, Understanding fractions of a whole and fractions as numbers

Numbers and the Number System 8, Using fraction notation to describe parts of a discrete set

Big Wheel

How this will help your child

- This activity will give your child a chance to make fractions using Numicon Shapes.
- It will help them to recognize and name fractions.
- It will allow them to practise writing fractions as numbers.

Words and phrases to use

fraction, part, whole, half, quarter, third, fifth, sixth, eighth, tenth, one part of..., two parts of...

You will need

- A pencil
- 1–6 dice

During the activity, look at what your child can do

- Make fractions by shading Shapes.
- Recognize and name some fractions.
- Write fractions as numbers.

What to do

- Give your child the Big Wheel sheet. Explain that there are 7 carriages on the big wheel. The holes in the Numicon Shapes show how many seats are in each carriage.
- Ask your child to look at the carriage containing the Numicon 2-shape and say how many seats are in the whole carriage. (Two.)
- Shade in 1 seat using a pencil and say that one seat in the carriage is taken. Ask your child what fraction of the carriage is taken.
- See if your child can use the phrases, 'one part of two' or 'one half'. Ask them to write this as a fraction in the box next to the carriage. **1**
- Take turns to roll the 1–6 dice to find out how many passengers are sitting in another carriage. For example, if the dice shows 5, then 5 passengers could be shaded in on the 8-shape carriage.
- Ask your child to describe how many seats in the carriage are full and to write and say the fraction, e.g. 'five parts of eight' or 'five eighths'. **2**
- Repeat until all carriages have some passengers.

> ### Next steps...
> - Ask, 'What fraction of the seats in each carriage are empty?' and, 'Are any carriages half full?'
> - Use items in sets, e.g. eggs in boxes or cakes in packets, to describe fractions.

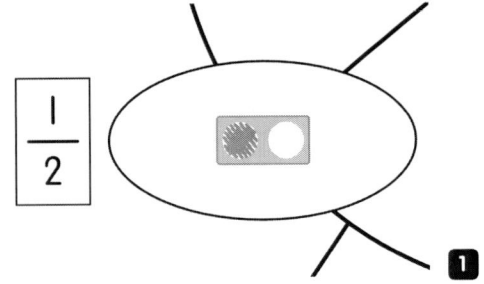

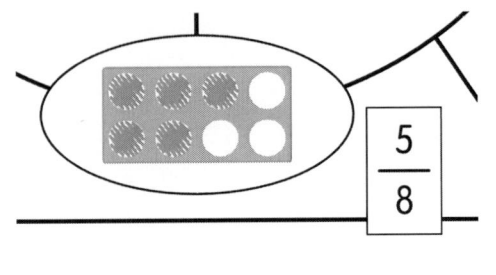

Name ....

Date .... / .... / ....

Big Wheel

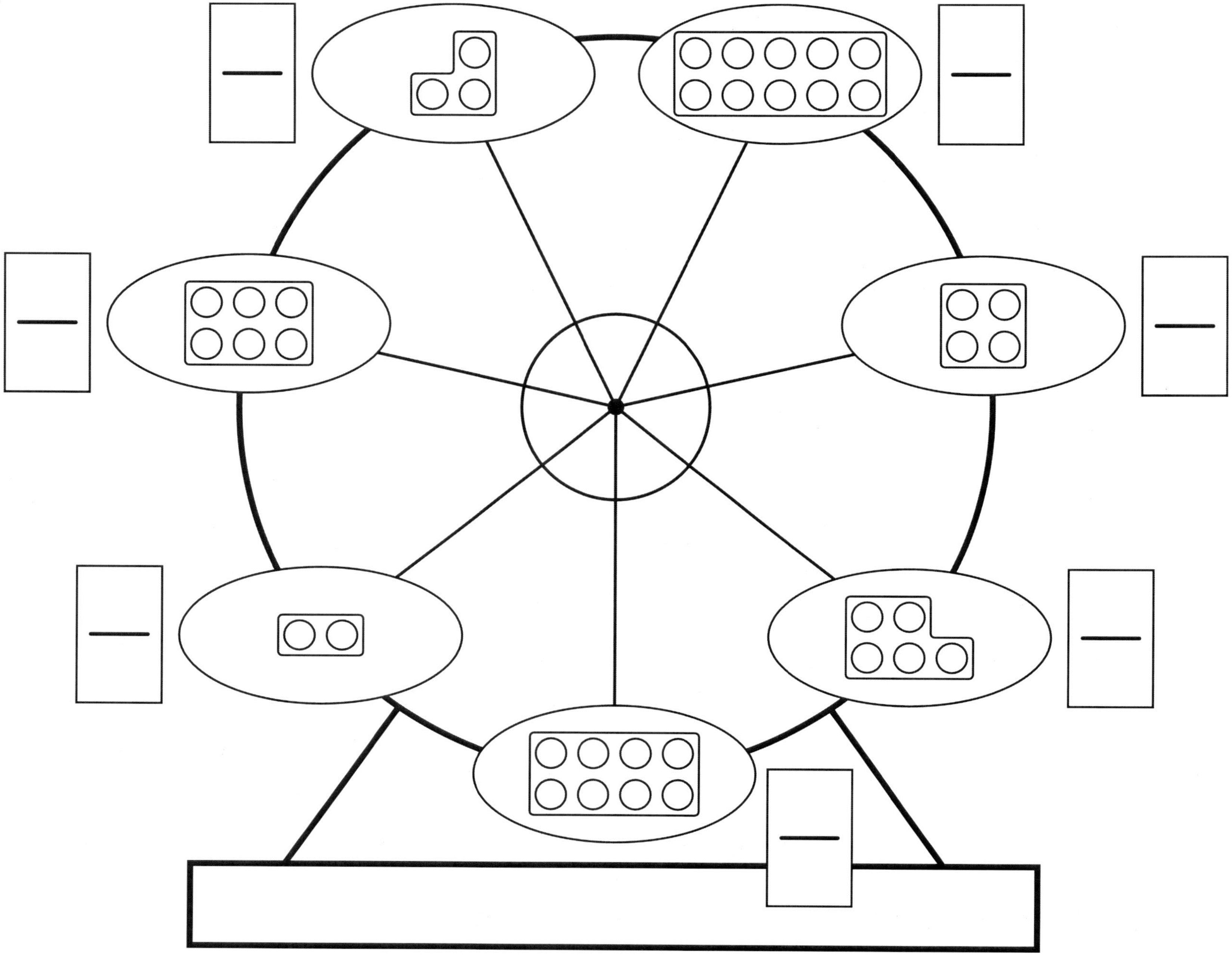

Number, Pattern and Calculating 3
Numbers and the Number System 8, Using fraction notation to describe parts of a discrete set

Calculating 1, Developing fluency with adding and subtracting facts to 10

Around The Board

How this will help your child

- This activity will allow your child to practise adding small numbers by looking for patterns.
- It will give them a chance to use number patterns up to 10.
- It will help them to understand that a list of numbers can be totalled in any order.

Words and phrases to use

add, plus, total, compare, estimate, group, organize, pattern, combine, score

You will need

- 2 counters (one colour for each player)
- A pencil
- 1–6 dice

During the activity, look at what your child can do

- Make reasonable estimates (not guesses) of the total list of small numbers.
- Remember adding facts up to 10 to help group numbers into 10s.
- Talk about patterns in the Numicon Shapes and relate these to totals.
- Know that numbers can be totalled in any order.

What to do

- Give your child the Around The Board sheet. Both players choose a counter to use.
- Decide your starting place by putting a counter on any number card.
- Write this first number on the number list next to the board. **1**
- Take it in turns to roll the dice. Move in any direction and write the number you land on to your list.
- Repeat until each player has 5 numbers.
- The winner is the person with the highest total score.
- Ask your child to decide who has won the game by comparing the numbers in the lists. Encourage your child to estimate the total.
- Ask your child to calculate the total. Look for pairs of numbers that can be grouped to make 10s, rather than adding the numbers in the order they are written in each list. **2**

Next steps…

- Set a target total. The winner is the person who gets closest to this score.
- Play a shopping game. Label goods with whole number prices, e.g. £1 to £9. Give your child an amount to spend. They can make lists, estimate and calculate totals.

Number list

Player 1	Player 2
4	
3	
6	
1	
7	
21	

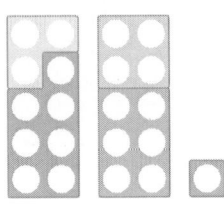

Number list

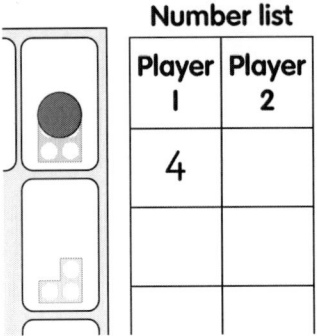

Player 1	Player 2
4	

1

2

Name .... Date .... / .... / ....

Around The Board

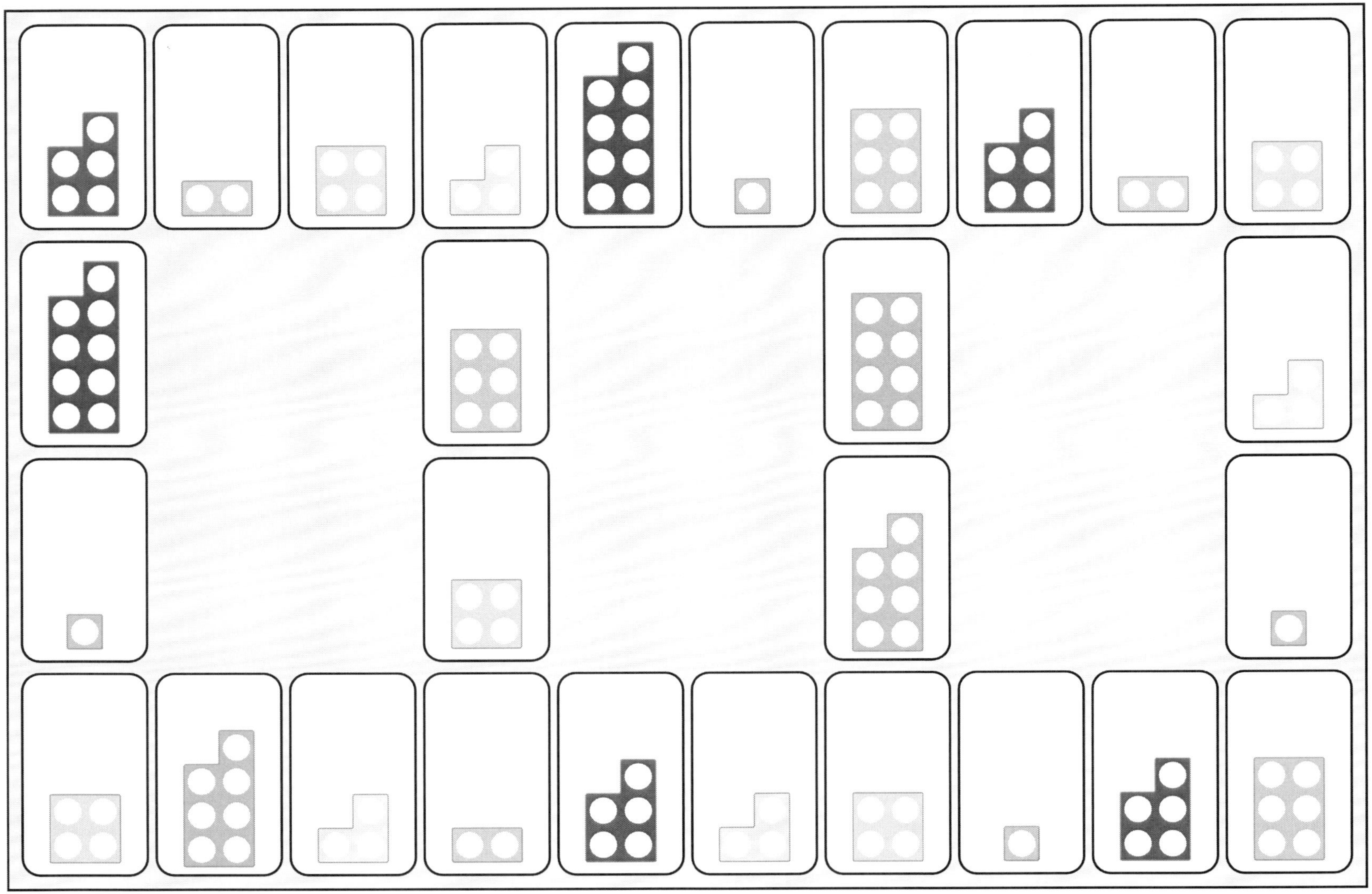

Player 1	Player 2

Number list

Calculating 2, Developing fluency with adding and subtracting facts to 20

Total 20

How this will help your child

- This activity will give your child a chance to recall and practise adding facts of 20.
- It will help them to notice patterns in the Numicon Shapes.

Words and phrases to use

add, equals, adding facts, total, pattern

You will need

- Scissors

During the activity, look at what your child can do

- Recall number facts to 20.
- Use Numicon Shape patterns to see numbers.

What to do

- Give your child the Total 20 sheet and ask them to look at the two Numicon 10-shapes at the top of the sheet and to describe what they can see.
- Agree that these two 10-shapes placed together show the number 20.
- Ask your child to look at the rest of the Shapes on the sheet and see if they notice any patterns in the numbers.
- Encourage your child to see how 2 cards next to each other add to make a total of 20, e.g. 12 + 8. **1**
- Help your child to cut along the dotted lines to make 20 cards.
- Shuffle the cards and place them picture side up.
- Ask your child to pick a card and to say the number out loud, e.g. 'thirteen'.
- Ask them to find the number that adds to 13 to make a total of 20.
- If your child is unsure, ask them to put their card below the two Numicon 10-shapes to help them see the number needed. **2**
- Encourage your child to say the adding fact out loud, e.g. 'thirteen add seven makes twenty.'
- Continue until all the cards are in pairs.

> ### Next steps...
> - Play with a timer – how fast can you find all the pairs and say the number facts?
> - Lay the cards picture side down. Turn over two cards. Do they show a total of 20? If yes, then put them in a pair. If not, put both cards back face down.

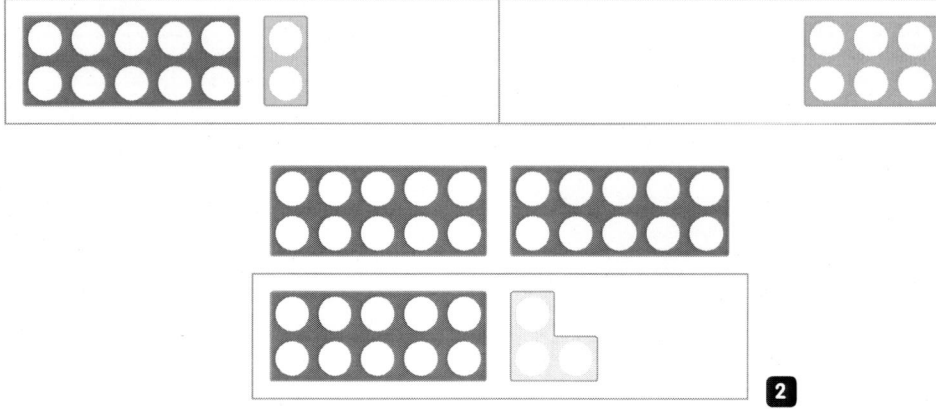

Total 20

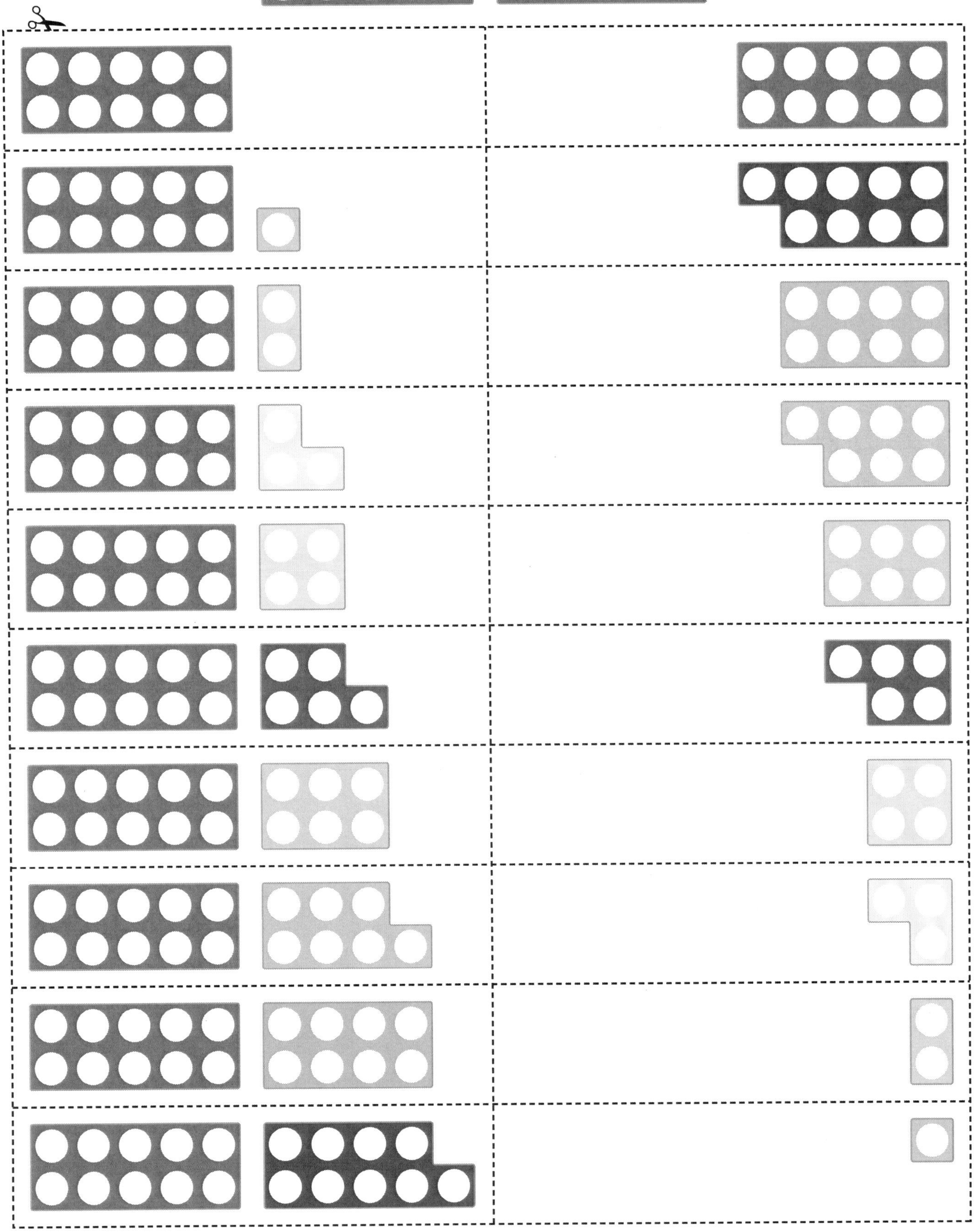

Calculating 3, Mental methods for adding single-digit numbers

Climb The Stairs

How this will help your child

- This activity will help your child to understand the close relationship between 9 and 10 when adding 9 to other numbers.
- It will allow them to practise adding 9 to numbers, by adding 10 and then making the total 1 fewer.

Note: encourage children to practise their adding in different ways than just 'counting on'. Help them to see that, e.g. adding 9 is easier if you add 10 and subtract 1.

Words and phrases to use

different, add, one fewer, adjust

You will need

- Coloured pencils (6 colours)
- An eraser

During the activity, look at what your child can do

- Add 9 to 1- and 2-digit numbers in their head without counting.

What to do

- Give your child the Climb The Stairs sheet.
- Explain that the postal worker has to deliver mail to every ninth flat in the block of flats. The lift has broken, so the only way to get to the other floors is to climb the stairs.
- Choose any door number on the ground floor. Ask your child what would be the next flat that the postal worker had to deliver to.
- Encourage your child to add 9 to this number and ask them to talk about how they are adding 9, e.g. by adding 10 and then subtracting 1.
- Your child should get the postal worker to climb to the top floor by adding 9 to each new number and using a coloured pencil to draw on each door the postal worker stopped at, e.g. 1 + 9 = 10, 10 + 9 = 19, 19 + 9 = 28. **1**
- Record the adding sentences. **2**
- Erase the adding sentences and repeat with a different ground floor door number and a different coloured pencil.

Next steps...

- Draw all the possible routes from the ground floor using 6 different coloured pencils. Talk with your child about any patterns they can see.
- Look at the list of totals for the adding sentences. Talk with your child about any patterns they can see, e.g. 1, 10, 19, 28, 37, 46, 55.

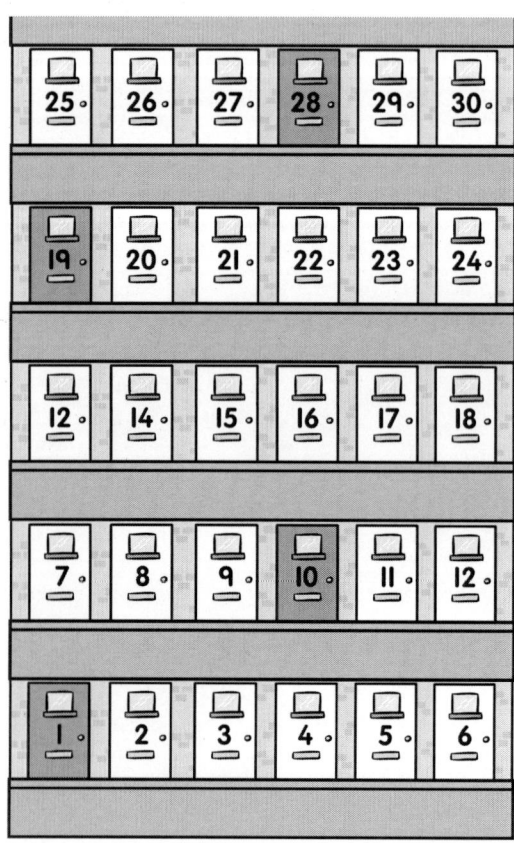

1

$$1 + 9 = 10$$

$$10 + 9 = 19$$

$$19 + 9 = 28$$

2

Climb The Stairs

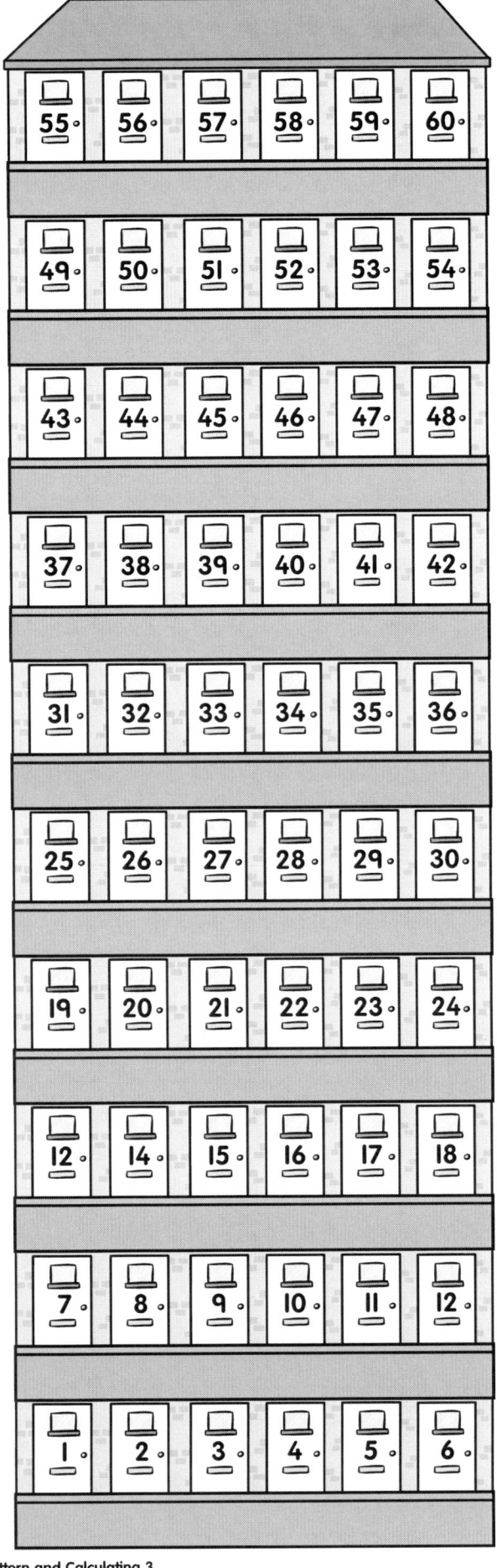

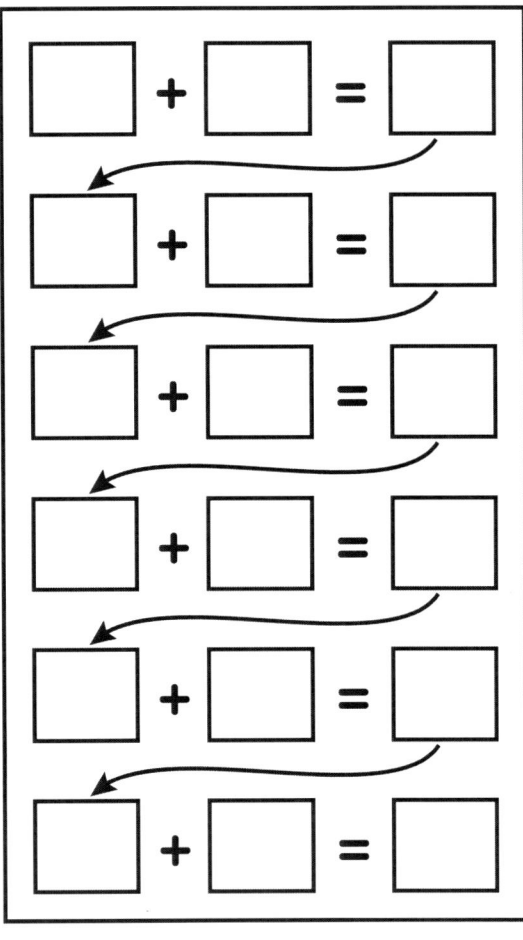

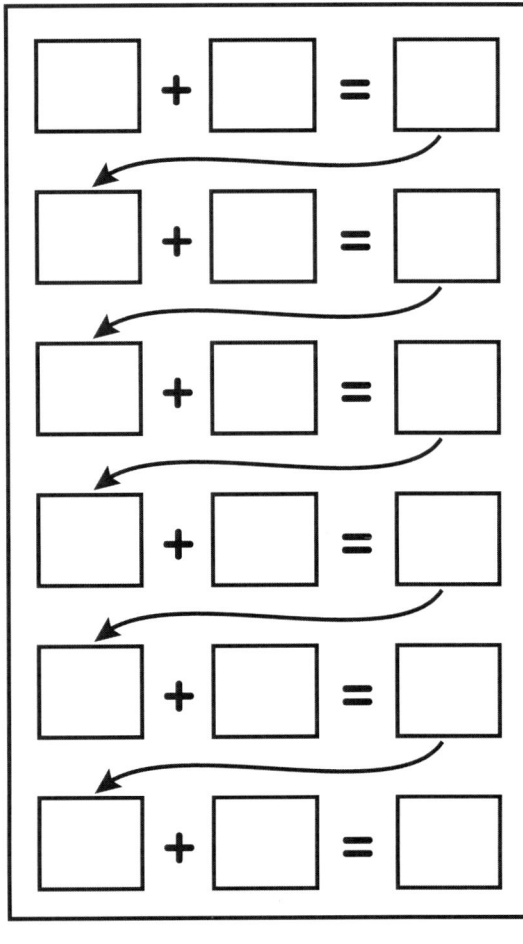

Calculating 4, Mental methods for subtracting single-digit numbers

Market Stall

How this will help your child

- This activity will help your child use subtracting facts of numbers to 10 when taking away from multiples of ten.
- It will allow them to use Numicon Shape patterns to subtract numbers without counting.

Words and phrases to use

subtracting, take away, fewer, pattern, multiples

You will need

- A pencil
- A paper clip
- Card Numicon 10-shapes

During the activity, look at what your child can do

- Subtract 1-digit numbers from multiples of 10 without counting.
- Use Numicon Shape patterns to see numbers.

What to do

- Give your child the Market Stall sheet and use the pencil and paper clip to make the spinner.
- Make the spinner by placing the paper clip over the centre spot of the spinner. Push the tip of the pencil through the centre spot and hold it in place as you spin the paper clip.
- Ask your child to choose a stall and use their card Numicon 10-shapes to show the number of items available on their chosen stall, e.g. 90 apples. **1**
- Tell your child that they need to spin the spinner to see how many of the items on their stall are being bought, e.g. 4 apples.
- Ask your child to work out how many apples are left on the stall. They might want to cover 4 holes on the final 10-shape to help them work this out. **2**
- The subtracting sentence can be written in the empty box beneath the stall. **3**
- Repeat for all the market stalls, spinning a new number of items to be bought each time.

> ### Next steps...
> - Look for multiples of 10 in daily life, e.g. on road signs, on car number plates. Ask your child to use these numbers to make their own subtracting stories.
> - Repeat the activity, but add 10 to each number on the spinner so that, e.g. '3' becomes '13'.

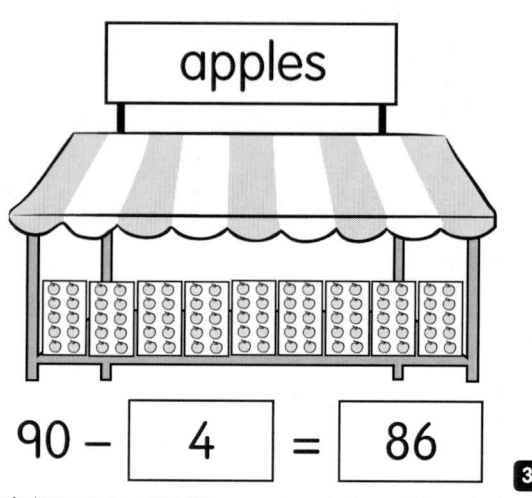

$$90 - \boxed{4} = \boxed{86}$$

3

Name ....

Date .... / .... / ....

Market Stall

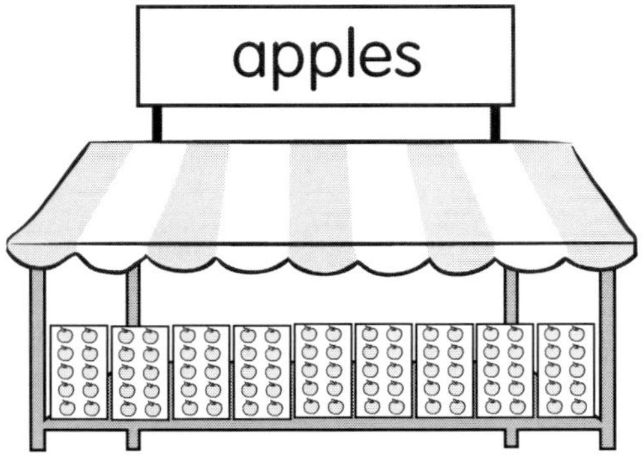

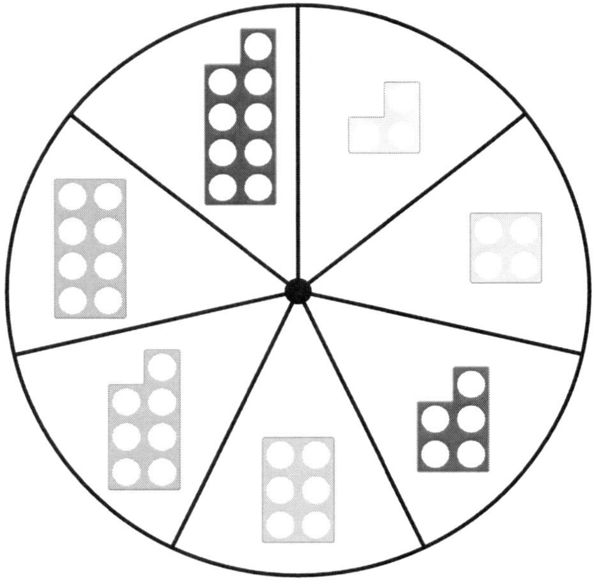

apples

90 − ☐ = ☐

cauliflowers

30 − ☐ = ☐

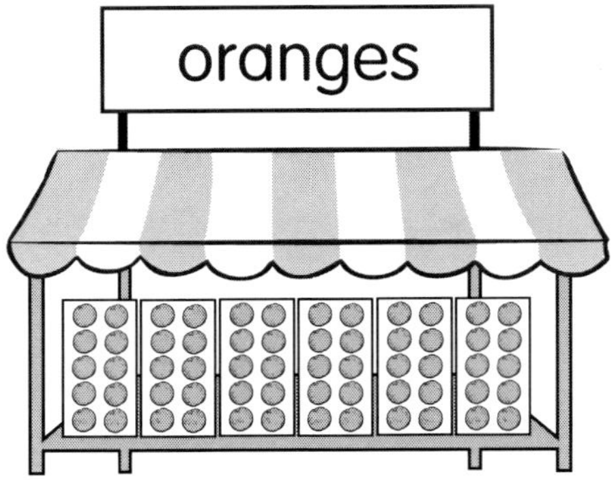

oranges

60 − ☐ = ☐

lettuces

40 − ☐ = ☐

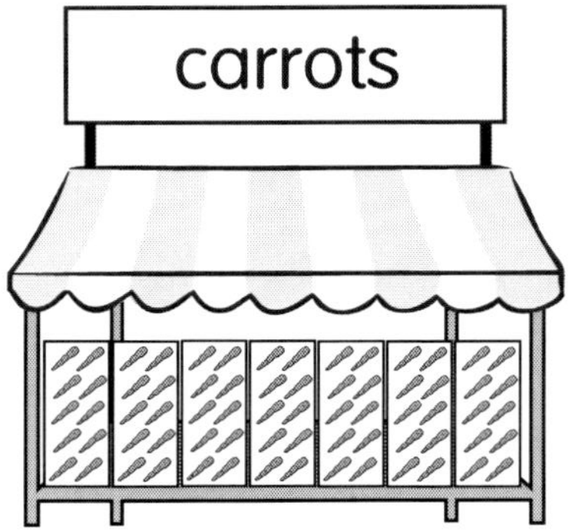

carrots

70 − ☐ = ☐

Pizza Maker

How this will help your child

- This activity will give your child a chance to discuss how the word 'times' is used in everyday life.

- It will help them to understand that 'times' means how often something is repeated.

Words and phrases to use

times, 'how many times', add, repeat, total, same

You will need

- A pencil
- Colouring pencils (optional)

During the activity, look at what your child can do

- Draw pictures to show repeated adding.
- Use the word 'times' to explain repeated adding.

What to do

- Give your child the Pizza Maker sheet.

- Talk about pizzas that are sold in shops and how the chef puts the same number of ingredients on every pizza so that they all look the same.

- Explain to your child that you want them to draw 3 pizzas that all look the same. The bases have already been drawn. Show your child that the chef has made a written record of this as '1 + 1 + 1 = 3'.

- Look at the list of ingredients for the different pizzas with your child.

- Ask them to choose 2 slices of chicken or 2 slices of egg to draw on every pizza. (Remember, all pizzas must look the same!)

- Ask your child, 'How many times did you draw 2 slices of chicken (or egg)?'

- Ask them to complete the table showing the ingredient they chose and the total. **1**

- Ask your child to draw the rest of the pizza and fill in the table by choosing the other ingredients. **2**

- Discuss the finished pizza by asking questions starting with, 'How many times…?'

Next steps…

- Ask your child to discuss how the totals for each ingredient might change if 4 or 5 pizzas were made.

- Ask your child to create their own pizza toppings for 3/4/5 pizzas that they would want to sell. Discuss the totals for each topping.

- Ice and decorate 3 or 4 biscuits with the same number of each item, e.g. 2 chocolate buttons, 3 jelly sweets.

Ingredients	Repeated adding sentances	Totals
Pizza base	1 + 1 + 1	= 3
Egg	2 + 2 + 2	= 6

1

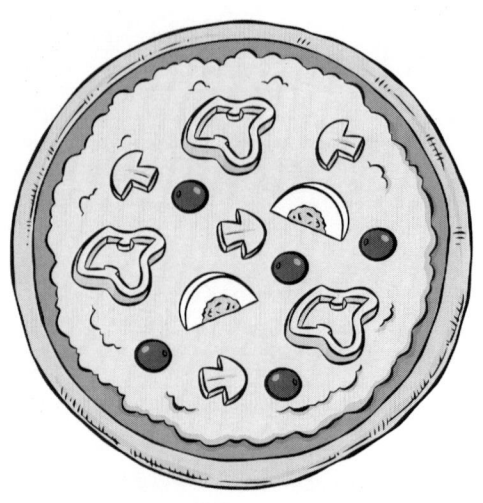

2

Name ....

Date .... / .... / ....

Pizza Maker

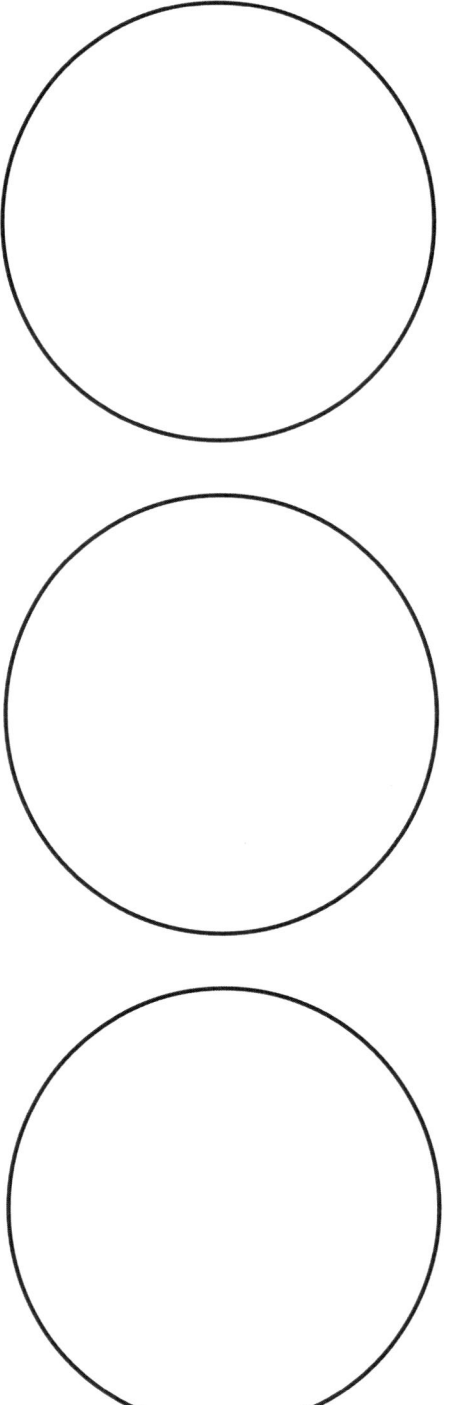

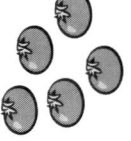

Menu

Each pizza must have:

2 slices of chicken

or

2 slices of egg

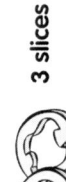 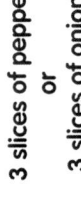 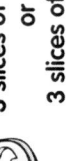

3 slices of pepper

or

3 slices of onion

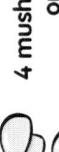 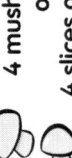 

4 mushrooms

or

4 slices of cheese

5 olives

or

5 cherry tomatoes

Ingredients	Repeated adding sentences	Totals
Pizza base	1 + 1 + 1	= 3
	2 + 2 + 2	

19

Calculating 6, Exploring multiplying through arrays

Sowing Seeds

How this will help your child

- It will allow your child to practise making arrays to show multiplication facts.
- It will help them to recall some multiplying facts.

Note: An array is a mathematical term that is used to describe a pattern of objects in rows of the same length.

Words and phrases to use

array, multiply, times, rows, equals

You will need

- 35 counters (or coins, buttons or pasta shapes to use as counters)
- Scissors

During the activity, look at what your child can do

- Build arrays accurately.
- Recall some multiplying facts.

What to do

- Give your child the Sowing Seeds sheet.
- Help them to cut out the 5 'seeds' cards and the 5 'rows of' cards. Shuffle the cards and put them face down in 2 separate piles.
- Ask your child to pick a 'rows of' card while you pick a 'seeds' card. Arrange these into a multiplying sentence, e.g. 3 rows of 2 seeds. **1**
- Now ask your child to make this array on the grid using counters to act as seeds. **2**
- Ask them to say the multiplying sentences out loud to describe the array, e.g. '3 rows of 2 seeds equals 6 seeds', '3 times 2 equals 6'.
- Pick another 'rows of' card and another 'seeds' card, then make and say this array.
- Continue until all the cards have been used.

Next steps...

- Play the game again, asking your child to predict the number of seeds needed before making the array.
- Challenge your child to look for arrays at home, e.g. egg boxes, window panes and telephone key pads.

| 3 rows of | 2 seeds | **1**

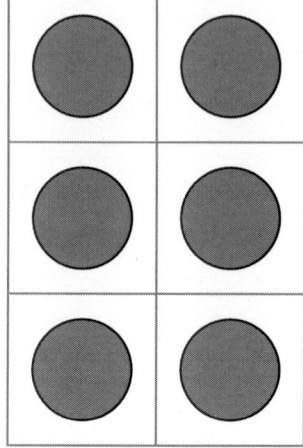

2

Sowing Seeds

Name ....

Date .... / .... / ....

	2 seeds
1 row of	3 seeds
2 rows of	4 seeds
3 rows of	5 seeds
4 rows of	6 seeds
5 rows of	

Number, Pattern and Calculating 3
Calculating 6, **Exploring multiplying through arrays**

Calculating 7, Introducing dividing as 'How many … in …?'

Mini Books

How this will help your child

- This activity will allow your child to practise finding how many groups are in a number.
- It will encourage them to use multiplication facts.

Words and phrases to use

'How many … in …?', multiplication fact, groups, grouping

You will need

- Coloured pencils
- A sheet of paper
- Scissors

During the activity, look at what your child can do

- Group objects to show 'How many groups are in …?'
- Use multiplying facts and Numicon Shape patterns to show the grouping.

What to do

- Give your child the Mini Books sheet.
- Ask your child to look at the sheets of paper and describe the sheets. They may say '6 rows of 4 sheets' or '4 rows of 6 sheets'.
- Help your child to cut out the sheets and ask them to group them into mini books, e.g. 6 books of 4 sheets or 4 books of 6 sheets. **1**
- Help your child to cut out the Numicon Shape cards from the Mini Books sheet. Shuffle them and place them face down.
- Ask your child to choose a Shape card. This is the number of sheets needed to make new mini books, e.g. 8.
- Ask your child to make mini books that each have 8 sheets of paper. How many can they make from their 24 sheets of paper? **2**
- Ask your child to say the sentence out loud, e.g. 'How many 8s are in 24?'
- Choose a different card for a different number of sheets per mini book. Make the mini books and say the sentence out loud.
- Encourage your child to predict how many groups can be made by using their multiplication facts, e.g. 'If there are 8 sheets in a book, $3 \times 8 = 24$, so 3 mini books can be made.'

Next steps…

- Make books with 16 or 18 mini sheets instead of 24. Are there any Shape cards that cannot be used without having some sheets left over?
- Plan a meal for friends, e.g. 'If we had 30 fish fingers, how many children could we invite if they all ate 3 fish fingers each? What if they ate 5 fish fingers each?' Draw pictures to show the 30 fish fingers grouped on the plates.

Mini Books

sheets in
each book

sheets in
each book

sheets in
each book

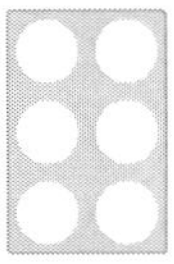

sheets in
each book

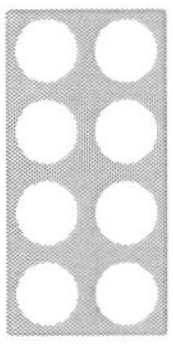

sheets in
each book

Money Box

How this will help your child

- This activity will give your child a chance to use adding and subtracting facts of 10 when adding and subtracting multiples of 10.
- It will help them to practise using maths words related to money.

Note: encourage your child to use variety in their spending stories so that they get the chance to use lots of maths words about money.

Words and phrases to use

add, subtract, 'how much less?', 'how much more?', spend, keep, pay, buy, take, save, give, put in

You will need

- Scissors
- A paper clip
- A pencil

During the activity, look at what your child can do

- Add and subtract multiples of 10.
- Use words related to money.

What to do

- Cut out the 10p coin cards from the Money Box sheet. Each player will need to choose one money box to play with.
- Ask your child to help you split the 10p coin cards equally between the two players so that each player has ten 10p coins.
- Each player starts by putting five coins in their money box. **1**
- Use the paper clip and pencil to spin for an amount of money by placing the paper clip over the centre spot of the spinner. Push the tip of the pencil through the centre spot and hold it in place as you spin the paper clip. Follow the instruction on the spinner, e.g. put 30p more into the money box. **2**
- Ask your child to tell you a story about their action, e.g. 'I had five 10p coins in my money box. I put in three more 10p coins from my pocket money. Now I have 80p altogether.'
- Take it in turns to spin the spinner. Encourage your child to use lots of different words and phrases in the stories.
- The money box cannot hold less than nothing or more than 100p. The winner is the first person to fill their money box completely.

> ### Next steps…
> - Play the game so the winner is the first to spend all the money in their money box.
> - Play a shopping game. Label goods with prices that are multiples of 10p. Your child can work out the change from 100p.

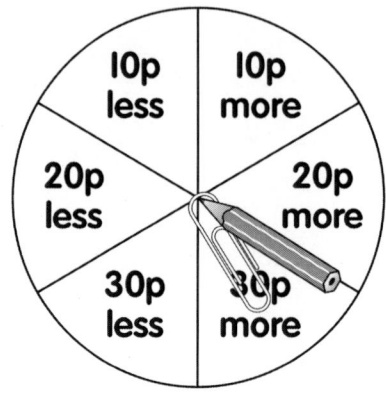

Name ....

Date .... / .... / ....

Money Box

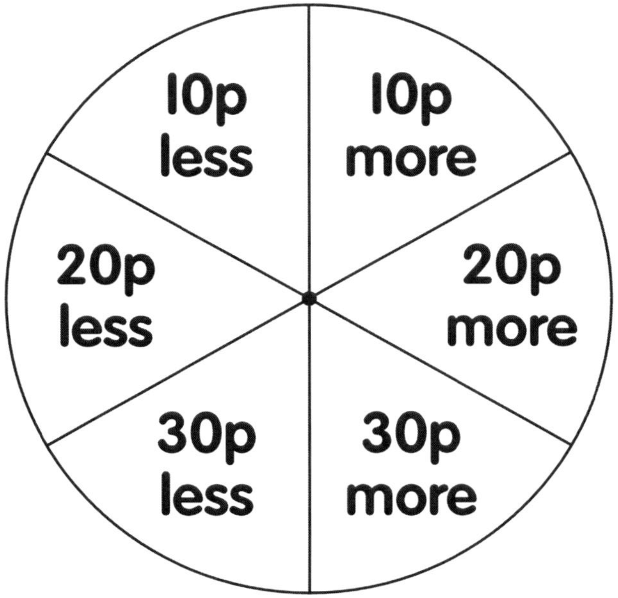

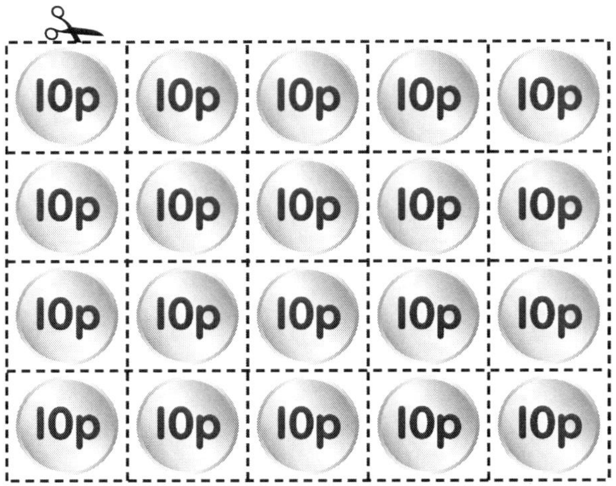

10p 10p 10p 10p
10p 10p 10p 10p
10p 10p 10p 10p
10p 10p 10p 10p
10p 10p 10p 10p

10p more

20p more

30p more

30p less

20p less

10p less

Number, Pattern and Calculating 3
Calculating 8, Adding and subtracting multiples of 10 and 100

Domino Doubles

How this will help your child

- It will help your child to practise doubling and halving 2-digit numbers.
- It will give them a chance to look for number patterns that are similar to help with doubling and halving.

Words and phrases to use

doubles, halves, similar, pattern

You will need

- Scissors

During the activity, look at what your child can do

- Double and halve some 2-digit numbers.
- Notice and use similar patterns.

What to do

- Cut out the dominoes from the Domino Doubles sheet and place them face up.
- Ask your child to find a domino showing the Numicon 10-pattern.
- Now ask them to find a domino that shows double 10 and put the two dominoes together. **1**
- Ask your child to find a domino showing the Numicon 22-pattern.
- Now ask them to find a domino that shows half of 22 and put the two dominoes together. **2**
- Play a game of dominoes where you have to match Numicon Shape patterns to their doubles or halves.
- Start with all the dominoes face down on the table. Each player takes 5 dominoes.
- Take it in turns to place a domino face up next to one already used in the game.
- After each turn, pick up another face down domino until there are none left.
- If a player cannot go they should pick up a domino and miss their turn.
- The winner is the first to put down all of their dominoes.

> ### Next steps…
> - Write the numbers on the back of the dominoes and play the game using these instead of the Numicon Shape patterns.
> - Practise doubling and halving 2-digit numbers on doors, buses, shop signs.

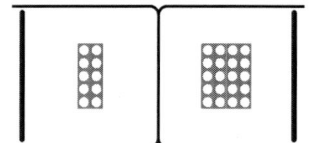

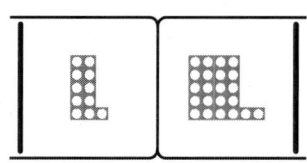

Name ....

Date .... / .... / ....

Domino Doubles

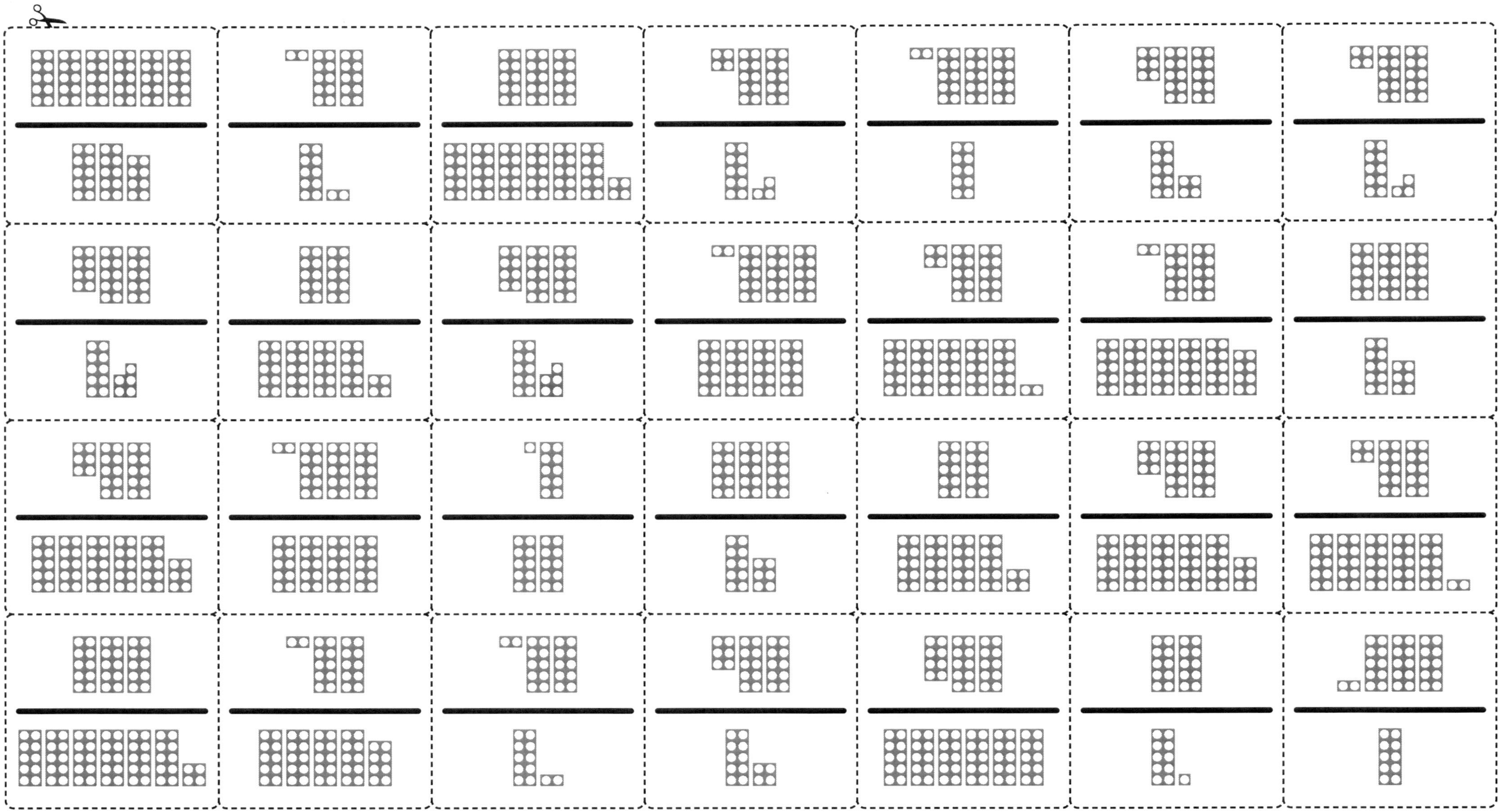

Calculating 10, Learning multiplying facts and looking for patterns

Frog Hop

How this will help your child

- This activity will allow your child to recognize numbers that are multiples of 2 and multiples of 10.
- It will help them to recall part of the 2 times table.

Words and phrases to use

multiple, times table, pattern

You will need

- 1–6 dice
- 2 counters

During the activity, look at what your child can do

- Recall part of the 2 times table.
- Recognize that multiples of 10 are also multiples of 2.
- See some patterns of multiples in part of a hundred square.

What to do

- Give your child the Frog Hop sheet and ask them to look at the lily pads and to show you numbers in the 2 times table (multiples of 2) and/or the 10 times table (multiples of 10).
- To begin, each player puts a counter on the frog at the start.
- Each frog counter hops in multiples of 2.
- Roll the dice to find out the number of hops the frog takes, e.g. if the dice shows 4, then 4 times 2 hops equals 8. Move the frog to the number 8 lily pad. **1**
- Take it in turns to roll the dice and to move the frogs through the pond of lily pads.
- Encourage your child to make the frog hop in 2s, rather than counting in ones.
- If a frog finishes on a multiple of 10, they can hop to the next multiple of 10. **2**
- The winner is the first frog to land on the reeds next to the number 60 lily pad.

> ### Next steps…
> - Play the game so that the frogs have to hop in multiples of 4.
> - Then play the game so that the frogs have to hop in multiples of 3.

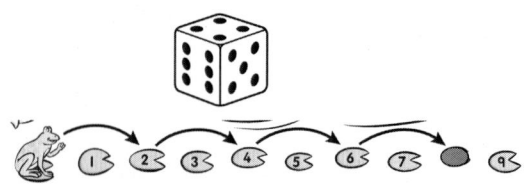

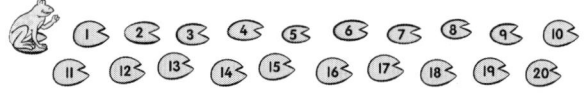

Name ....

Date .... / .... / ....

Frog Hop

Number, Pattern and Calculating 3
Calculating 10, Learning multiplying facts and looking for patterns

Calculating 11, Introducing the sharing structure of dividing

Picnic Basket

How this will help your child

- This activity will give your child practice in sharing amounts.
- It will help them use maths words linked to sharing.
- It will show them how the ÷ symbol is used in a division sentence.

Words and phrases to use

shared between, shared equally, divided between, divided, each

You will need

- 25 counters or buttons

During the activity, look at what your child can do

- Show 'sharing' using counters or buttons.
- Say dividing sentences to explain sharing.
- Recognize and use the ÷ symbol.

What to do

- Give your child the Picnic Basket sheet.
- Look at the 4 picnic baskets and talk about the food items in each one.
- Ask your child to choose a picnic basket, look at the picnic list and choose one item from the basket, e.g. lemon cupcakes.
- Explain that the item they have chosen needs to be shared equally onto the plates of the number of people at the picnic, e.g. 6 lemon cupcakes among 3 people.
- Ask your child to collect the correct number of counters to represent the item and then to share the items equally on their plates. **1**
- Encourage them to say what they have done, e.g. 'six lemon cupcakes shared between three plates gives two lemon cupcakes each', and 'six divided by three equals two' (6 ÷ 3 = 2).
- Collect the counters and choose a different food item from the basket to share among the plates, e.g. 18 blueberries. **2**
- Once you have finished sharing the food items from one basket, you can try different picnic baskets.

Next steps…

- Practise sharing amounts with your child in everyday life, e.g. when serving a meal or playing a board game.
- Play a 'Would you rather have…?' game, e.g. 8 sweets shared between 2 or 12 sweets shared between 4?

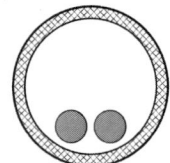
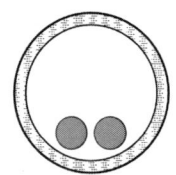

1

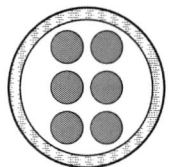
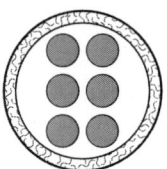
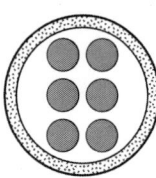

2

Name ....

Date .... / .... / ....

Picnic Basket

Picnic for 3

15 egg sandwiches
6 lemon cupcakes
18 blueberries
9 cucumber sticks

Picnic for 4

20 tuna sandwiches
8 strawberry cupcakes
24 raspberries
16 pepper sticks

Picnic for 2

8 cheese sandwiches
4 chocolate cupcakes
12 strawberries
10 carrot sticks

Picnic for 5

20 chicken sandwiches
10 vanilla cupcakes
25 grapes
15 celery sticks

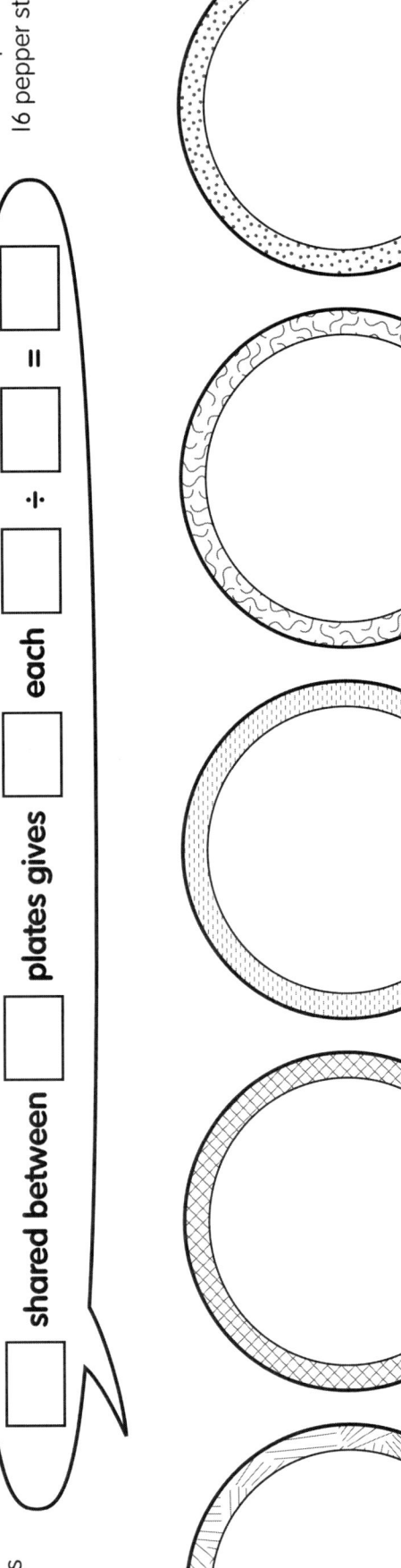

☐ shared between ☐ plates gives ☐ each   ☐ ÷ ☐ = ☐

Numicon: Number, Pattern and Calculating 3
Calculating 11, Introducing the sharing structure of dividing

25

Raffle Tickets

How this will help your child

- This activity will give your child a chance to partition when adding 2-digit numbers.
- It will encourage them to estimate totals when adding 2-digit numbers.

Words and phrases to use

add, partition, tens, units, estimate, total

You will need

- Scissors

During the activity, look at what your child can do

- Partition and add some 2-digit numbers.
- Make sensible estimates of totals.

What to do

- Help your child to cut out the 20 raffle tickets from the Raffle Tickets sheet.
- Choose a ticket and ask your child if they can split the number into tens and units, e.g. 13 is 1 ten and 3 units.
- To play the game, spread out all the tickets face down. The aim is to pick two tickets, add them together and reach a target total.
- Give your child a target total to aim for, e.g. 'less than 65'.
- Ask your child to select 2 tickets to add together. **1**
- Encourage your child to estimate if the total of the 2 tickets will be under or over the target total.
- Ask your child to split the numbers into tens and units, e.g. '15 is 1 ten and 5 units, 23 is 2 tens and 3 units'.
- Add the units together and add the tens together, before finding the total. **2**
- If the total fits with the target total, they can keep the tickets. If not, the tickets should be put back face down.
- Take it in turns to play the game until all tickets have been used.

> ### Next steps…
> - Play a different game by starting with all the cards face up. Give your child a narrower target total, e.g. 'between 25 and 55', 'between 45 and 65', 'between 85 and 95'. Ask your child to select two cards that, when added together, will meet the target total.
> - Play either game with 3 tickets.

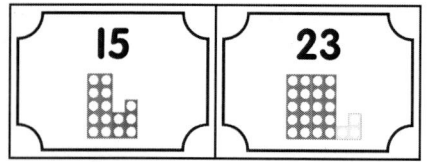 **1**

 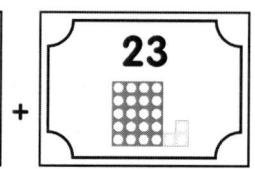 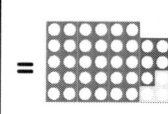 **2**

Name ....

Date .... / .... / ....

Raffle Tickets

Calculating 13, Using apparatus and imagery to introduce the written column method for adding

Treasure Chest

How this will help your child

- This activity will allow your child to partition numbers that are too big to add in their head.
- It will help them to see how a column method can be useful when adding large numbers.

Words and phrases to use

hundreds, tens, units, column method, partition, regroup, total, estimate, range

You will need

- A paper clip
- A pencil

During the activity, look at what your child can do

- Make sensible estimates for a total.
- Partition 3-digit numbers.
- Regroup numbers to find a total.

What to do

- Give your child the Treasure Chest sheet and explain that the treasure chest can be opened using the 3-digit numbers on both locks.
- The aim is to spin the spinner to find a range for the total that will unlock the chest. Select one number from Lock A and one number from Lock B to add together. If the total is within the range on the spinner, the chest will open.
- Use the paper clip and pencil to make the spinner.
- Place the paper clip over the centre spot of the spinner. Push the tip of the pencil through the centre spot and hold it in place as you spin the paper clip. Spin the spinner to find a range for the total, e.g. 250 to 349.
- Ask your child to choose one number from Lock A and one number from Lock B to add together to fit within this range.
- Encourage your child to estimate the total before choosing to see if it is within the range on the spinner.
- Ask your child to separate these two numbers into the columns on the hundreds, tens and units grid. **1**
- Ask your child to regroup the hundreds together, the tens together and the units together to find the total. **2** If the total is within the range, the chest is unlocked!
- Spin again for a new range and choose new numbers for each lock.

Next steps…

- Work together to separate and regroup 3-digit numbers to find totals, e.g. the total mass of parcels for posting, or the total volume of liquid in a recipe.

	Hundreds	Tens	Units
Lock A	100	20	5
Lock B	200	10	3

1

	Hundreds	Tens	Units
Lock A	100	20	5
Lock B	200	10	3
	300	30	8

2

Name ....

Date .... / .... / ....

Treasure Chest

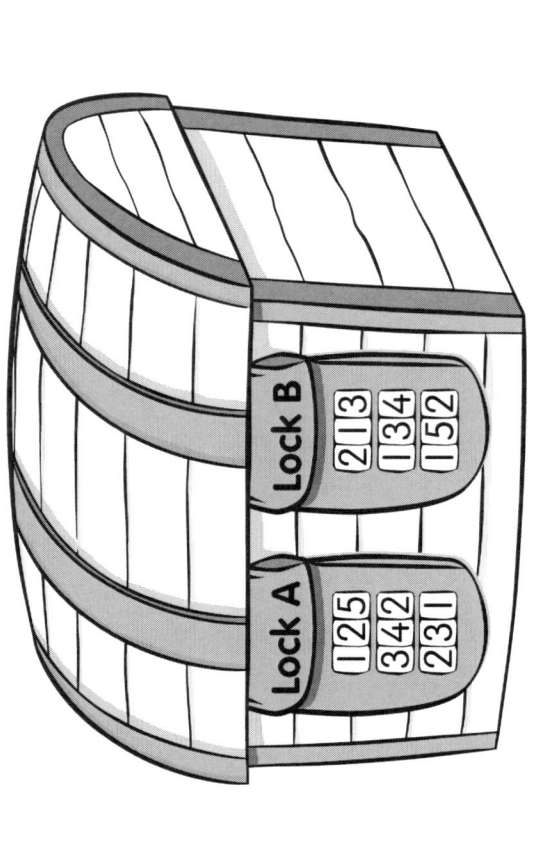

| | 350 to 449 | 450 to 549 |
| 250 to 349 | 550 to 649 | |

Lock A: 125, 342, 231

Lock B: 213, 134, 152

	Hundreds	Tens	Units
Lock A			
Lock B			

Numicon: Number, Pattern and Calculating 3
Calculating I3, Using apparatus and imagery to introduce the written column method for adding

Calculating 14, Using apparatus and imagery to support subtracting and introducing the written column method

Snail Race

How this will help your child

- This activity will give your child a chance to practise finding the difference between two numbers by adding or subtracting.
- It will help them to use number lines and record their ideas in number sentences.

Words and phrases to use

'how much further?', 'find the difference', add on, subtract, count back

You will need

- A paper clip
- A pencil

During the activity, look at what your child can do

- Find the difference between 100 and a 2-digit number using a number line.
- Write addition and subtraction sentences for finding the difference.

What to do

- Give your child the Snail Race sheet.
- Show your child the snails on the race tracks and discuss how they are lining up for a race.
- Explain that all the snails start at 0 and the aim is to finish at 100.
- Make the spinner in the Snail Race sheet using a paper clip and pencil. Place the paper clip over the centre spot of the spinner. Push the tip of the pencil through the centre spot and hold it in place as you spin the paper clip.
- Spin the spinner twice to find the distance that the first snail travels, e.g. spin 60 and then 3 to get 63.
- Ask your child to find where this number is on the race track number line and to write it in. **1**
- Ask your child to work out how much further the snail has to travel to reach the finish flag by finding the difference. **2**
- Encourage your child to say and write the addition and subtraction facts for finding the difference, e.g. 63 + 37 = 100, 37 + 63 = 100, 100 – 37 = 63, 100 – 63 = 37.
- Repeat with other snails by spinning for a new distance each time.

Next steps...

- Compare the distances of the snails, e.g. 'How much further would the first snail have to travel to have gone the same distance as the second snail?'
- Play numbered board games, e.g. Snakes and Ladders. Encourage your child to find the difference between their position on the board and the finishing square, or the next ladder up.

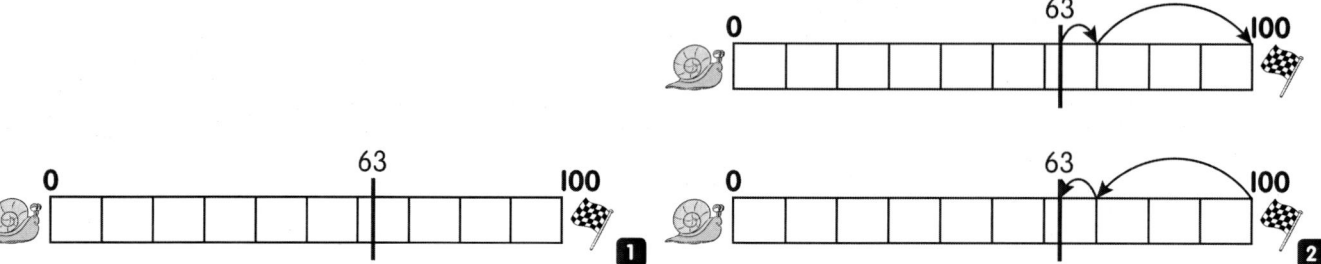

28

Name ....

Date .... / .... / ....

Snail Race

Spinner (circle divided into sections):

Outer ring: 10, 20, 30, 40, 50, 60, 70, 80, 90

Inner ring: 1, 2, 3, 4, 5, 6, 7, 8, 9

Race 1

100
100

□ + □ = 100

□ + □ = 100

100 − □ = □

100 − □ = □

0

Race 2

100
100

□ + □ = 100

□ + □ = 100

100 − □ = □

100 − □ = □

0

Race 3

100 
100

□ + □ = 100

□ + □ = 100

100 − □ = □

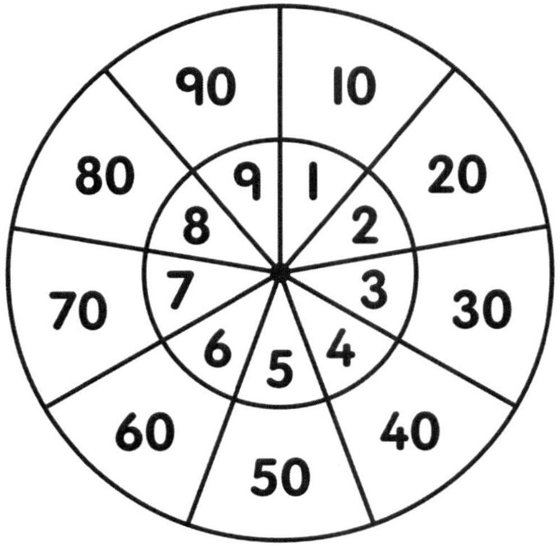

100 − □ = □

0

Number, Pattern and Calculating 3
Calculating 14, Using apparatus and imagery to support subtracting and introducing the written column method

Calculating 15, Exploring ratio and scaling problems and introducing the short written methods of multiplying and dividing

Seal Balance

How this will help your child

- This activity will help your child to understand how objects can be enlarged by multiplying.

- It will also give them the opportunity to use the phrase 'multiplied by' when describing patterns.

Words and phrases to use

multiplied by, 'how many times taller?', times, enlarge

You will need

- 1–6 dice

- A pencil

During the activity, look at what your child can do

- Draw a pattern and show how it has been multiplied.

- Use the phrase 'multiplied by' to describe how patterns increase in size.

What to do

- Give your child the Seal Balance sheet and explain to them that the seals are balancing towers of balls on their heads as part of their tricks for the sea-life show.

- These towers can be made taller depending on how good the seals are at balancing the balls.

- Ask your child to choose a seal and describe the patterns and number of balls in the seal's tower.

- Roll the dice to find out how good the seal is at balancing the balls, e.g. rolling a 3 will make the whole tower three times bigger.

- Ask your child to draw the complete tower on the seal's head. **1**

- Encourage them to describe what has happened to the pattern.

- Ask your child to complete the boxes in the multiplying sentence underneath the seal, showing how the tower has been made taller. **2**

- Repeat for the other seals in the sea-life show.

Next steps…

- Use coloured buttons or toy bricks to build simple patterns, then multiply the pattern by, e.g. 2, 3, 4.

- Set out a plate, glass and cutlery for a meal for one person. Use 'multiplied by' to describe how much would be needed if, e.g. 8 people were eating.

1

$1 \times \boxed{3} = \boxed{3}$ **2**

29

Name ....

Date .... / .... / ....

Seal Balance

1 × [ ] = [ ]

3 × [ ] = [ ]

2 × [ ] = [ ]

2 × [ ] = [ ]

Number, Pattern and Calculating 3
Calculating 15, Exploring ratio and scaling problems and introducing the short written methods of multiplying and dividing

Calculating 16, Making connections between dividing into equal parts and calculating with fractions

Hexagon Halving

How this will help your child

- This activity will give your child a chance to halve numbers that are multiples of 10.
- It will help them to see the link between halving and sharing into two equal parts.

Words and phrases to use

halve, half, share into equal parts

You will need

- 2 colours of counters or buttons (about 10 of each colour)
- Card Numicon Shapes (5-shape and 10-shape)

During the activity, look at what your child can do

- Share multiples of 10 into 2 equal parts.
- Understand how halving and sharing into 2 are the same action.

What to do

- Give your child the Hexagon Halving sheet.
- Explain that the aim is to build a path of counters across the board by moving from a hexagon to one next door.
- Ask your child to choose a hexagon on one side of the board.
- In order to be able to place a counter on the hexagon, they have to be able to halve the number.
- Encourage them to say the number sentence, e.g. 'half of 90 equals 45, 90 shared into 2 equal parts is 45'. If necessary, use card Numicon Shapes to help with the halving of numbers. **1**
- Once they have correctly halved the number, they can move to the next hexagon on the board.
- Your child can move in any direction, as long as the hexagons are touching each other. **2**
- The activity ends when the path of counters reaches the other side.

> ### Next steps…
> - Turn the activity into a game with 2 players where the aim is to get to the other side of the board before your opponent.
> - Add 100 to all the numbers on the game board. Encourage your child to halve the hundreds and then the tens.

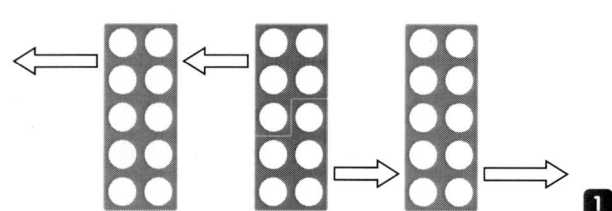

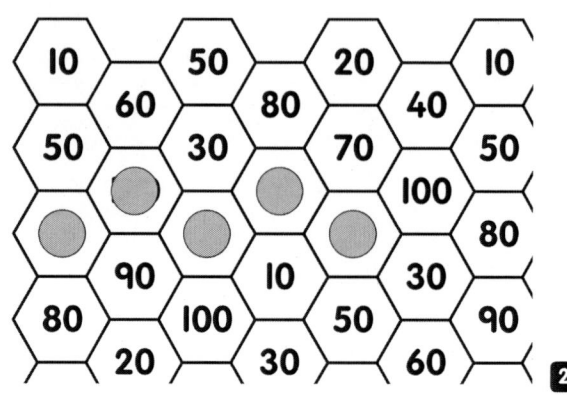

Name ....

Date .... / .... / ....

Hexagon Halving

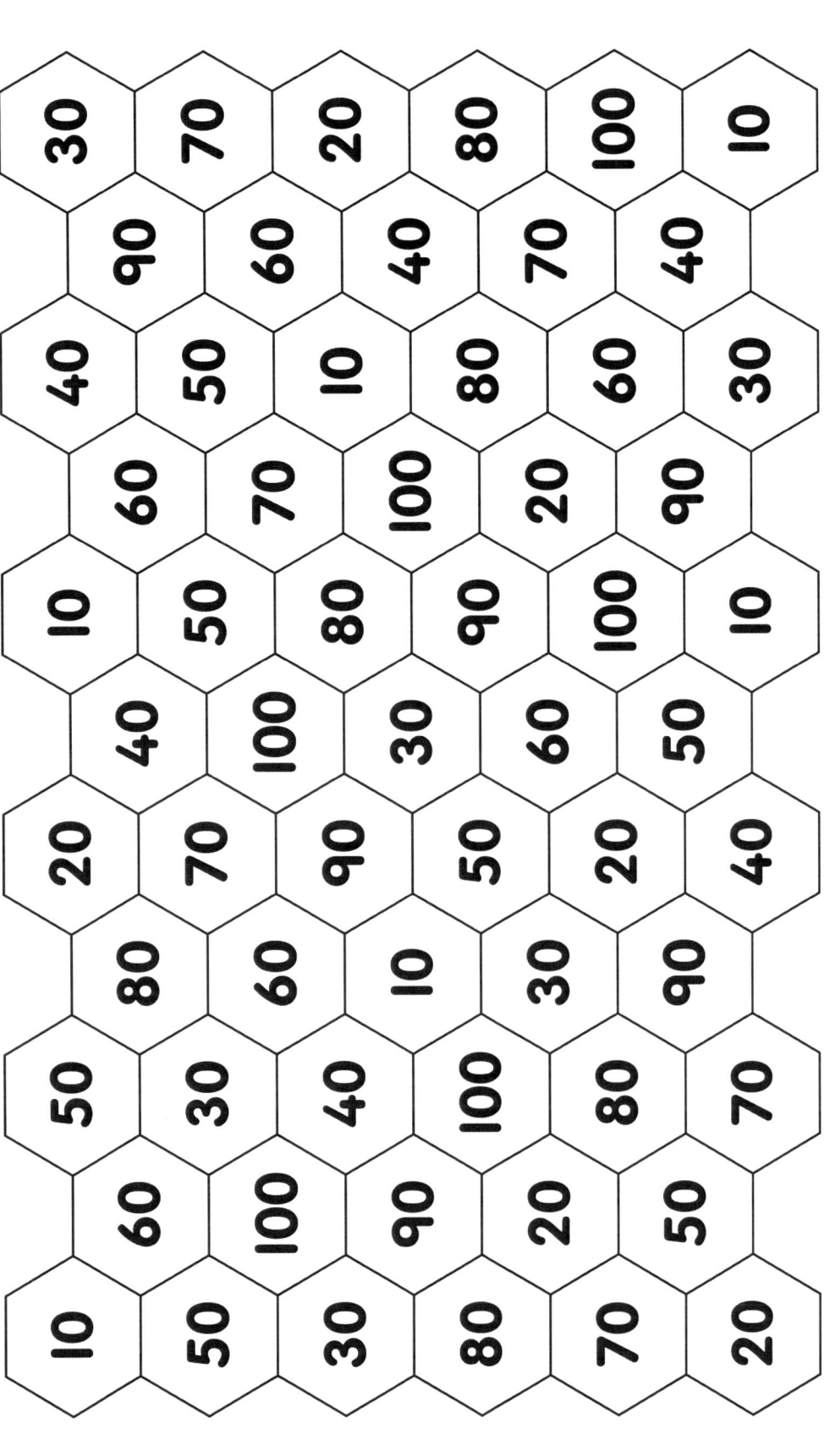

half of ☐ equals ☐ , ☐ shared into 2 equal parts is ☐

Number, Pattern and Calculating 3
Calculating 16, Making connections between dividing into equal parts and calculating with fractions

Card Numicon 1–10 Shapes

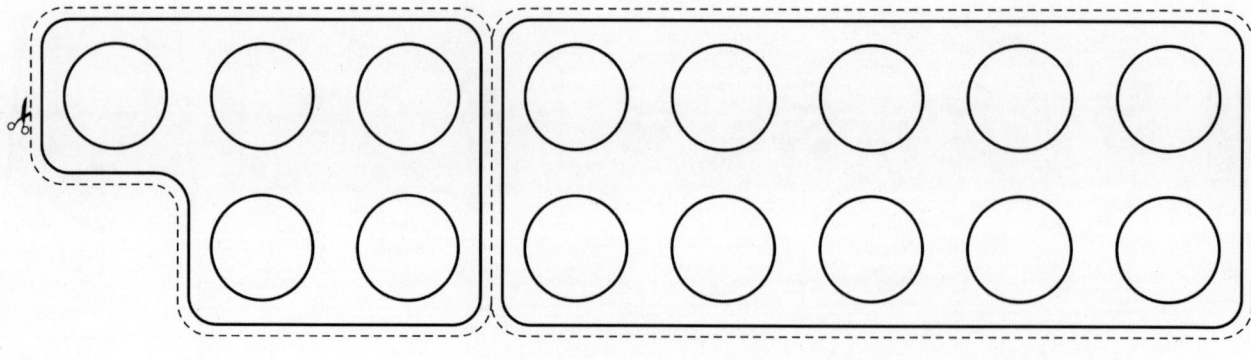

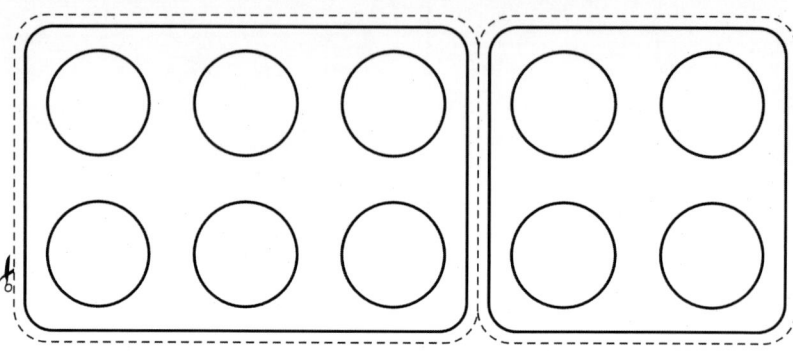

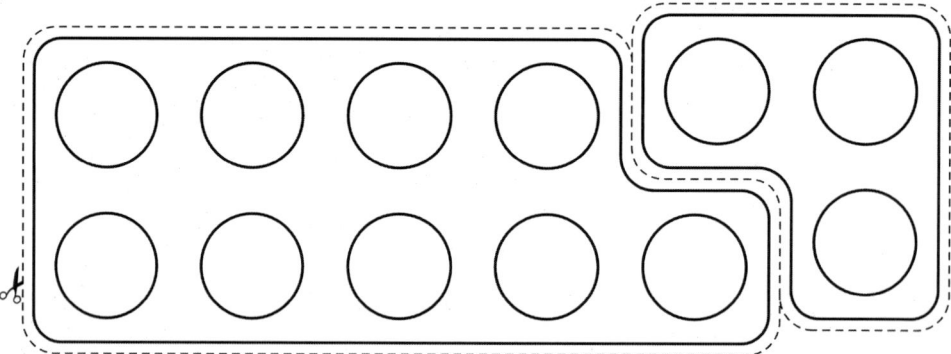

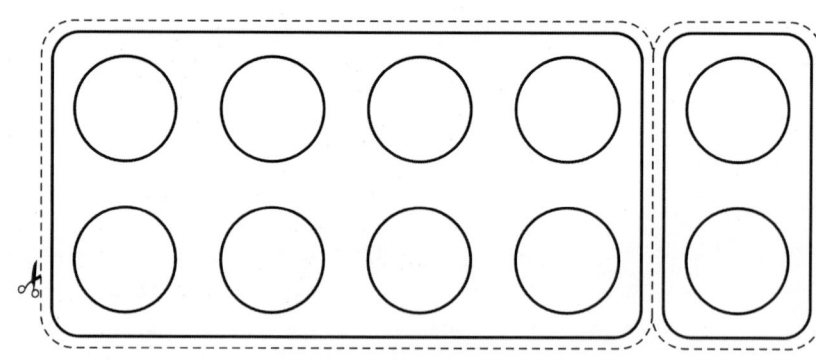

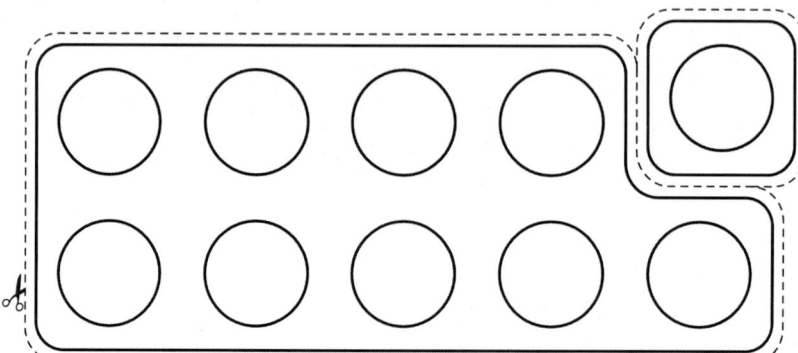

Name .... Date .... / .... / ....

Card Numicon 10-shapes

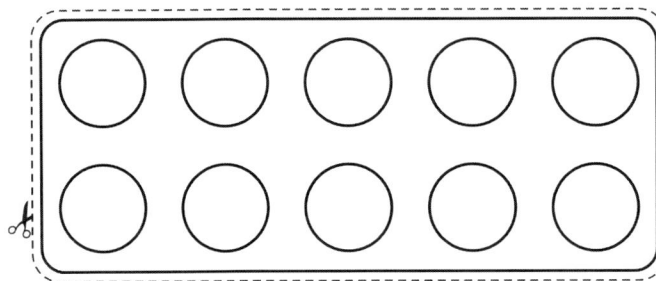 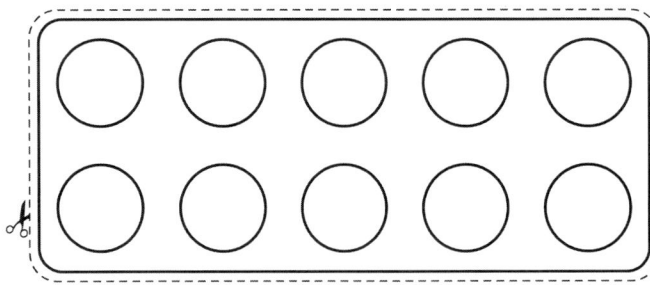

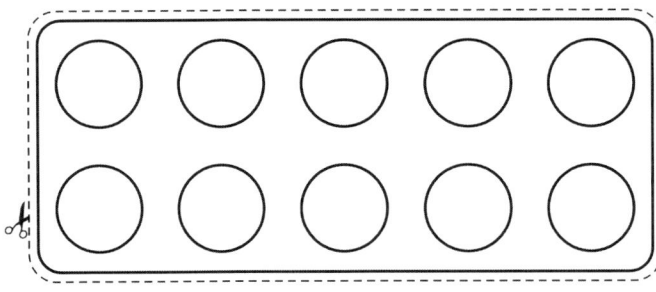 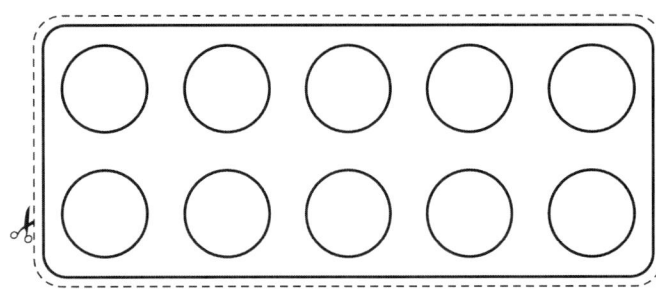

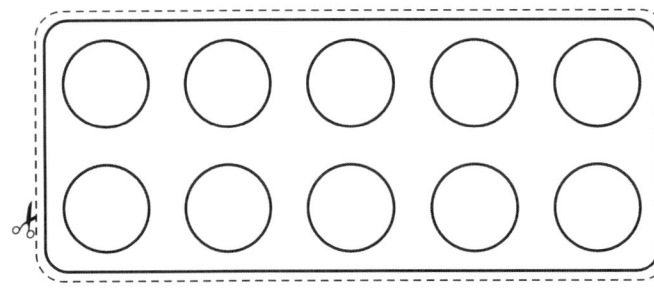 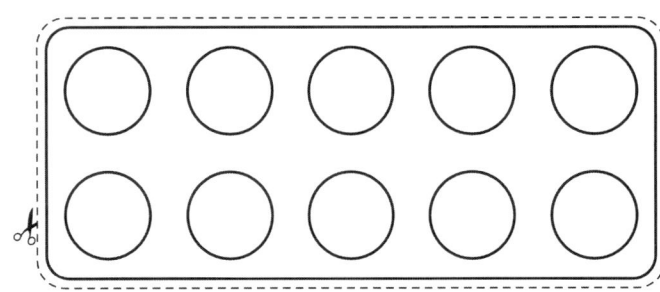

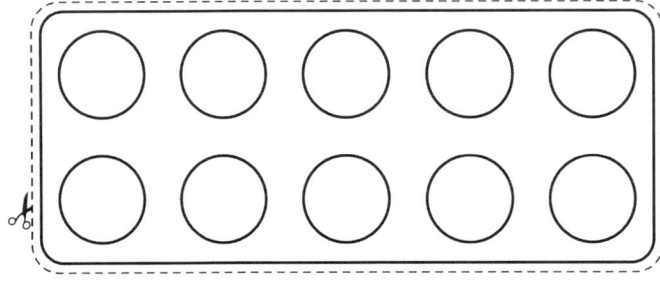 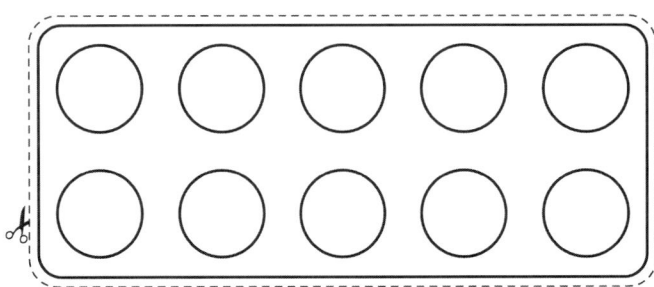

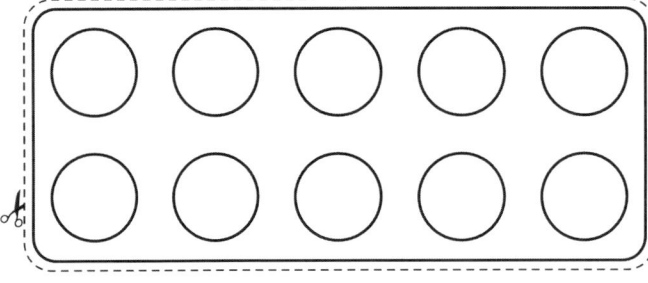 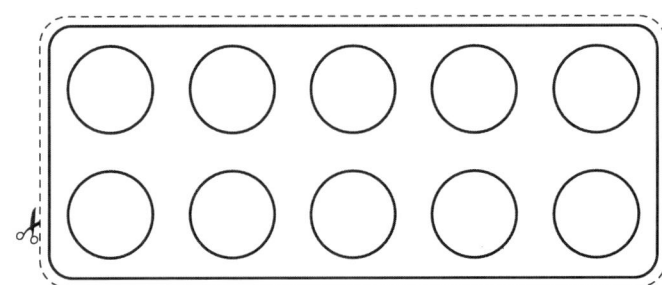

Number, Pattern and Calculating 3